Merry Christmas

Something for you to enjoy in Florida.

Love,

Louisa, Charlie, Margaret, Jim & Jem

NEEDLEWORK MASTERPIECES

NEEDLEWORK MASTERPIECES

20 Projects from the World's Great Museums

Melinda Coss

A Bulfinch Press Book
Little, Brown and Company
Boston · New York · Toronto · London

First North American Edition

ISBN 0-8212-2087-X

Library of Congress Catalog Card Number 94-75001

Bulfinch Press is an imprint and trademark of Little, Brown and Company (Inc.)

Published simultaneously in Canada by Little, Brown & Company (Canada) Limited

PRINTED IN ITALY

To the memory of Gwen George

CONTENTS

INTRODUCTION

Fine art has always influenced designers and the work of the great masters has been an irresistibly rich and exciting source of inspiration to many crafts people. Early pieces, worked in needlepoint and tapestry, such as the famous Bayeux tapestry, are established works of art in their own right and a number of the great masters featured in this book produced cartoons specifically for woven tapestries.

The fact of the matter is that painted canvases of famous masterpieces have been available from good needlework companies for at least two generations and this is because you have shown an insatiable appetite for stitching them. In the process of producing this book I was given permission to create charts from some of the most well loved canvases. Hals' *The Laughing Cavalier* was produced in printed canvas form by William Briggs Ltd, as was Millais' *Bubbles*, Leonardo's *The Last Supper*, Constable's *Flatford Mill* and Degas' *Ballet Rehearsal*. All proven favourites, they are shown here with the recipes for making them. Royal Paris in France were kind enough to provide the finished pieces for their *Floral Composition* and Renoir's *Woman with Dog*. The other interpretations in this book are of my own origination and are offered to you on the understanding that I have not attempted to replicate great works of art but merely to provide you with popular images, beloved by everybody, to re-create in stitches.

I have interpreted my colours as closely as I could to the inspirational works but you could, of course, create your own colour schemes for the designs. The idea to keep with you is that needlepoint is a pleasurable and therapeutic occupation, so allow yourself as much leeway as you like and do not be bothered about an odd stitch or two in the wrong place.

For appearances sake, many of the pieces in this book have been framed like the pictures they were taken from. However, you could make your needlepoint into a cushion cover, or mount your work of art on a screen, the panel of a door or a workbox. You could even stitch it to the back of a jacket. You can change the size of a finished piece so that it is either larger or smaller by selecting an alternative mesh size; the possibilities are endless if you treat these as basic designs ready for you to interpret in your own way.

On its own, needlepoint is not creative; it demands patience, neatness and a methodical approach. The creativity becomes evident in your selection of colours and the display of the final piece. No one piece is more difficult than another. Some, like Only Jesting, are a little fiddly because achieving a particular effect has necessitated lots of small areas of colour. Others, like Stoney Silence comprise large blocks of colour and will be quicker to stitch. One thing is for sure, when you have completed one piece of needlepoint successfully you will want to go on to another and hopefully, that will lead to you creating your own individual pieces from design to completion.

I hope that among this collection, you will find an interpretation of your favourite work of art. I hope also that this book provides you with the art of needlepoint and that you pass this skill down to your children and your children's children.

ANGELA

Inspired by *The Annunciation*, Fra Angelico (1387-1455)

The Annunciation by Fra Angelico (1387-1455)

Dominican Fra Angelico used his talent in the telling of the Christian story. His work, like the work of Leonardo, Raphael and Michelangelo, was strongly influenced by the Carmine frescoes. Fra Angelico's work rivalled that of his contemporary Giotto and his use of strong blues and pinks, coupled with his mastery of architectural perspective, gave his work a gentle intensity.

The inspiration for this design is drawn from the frescoes which Angelico painted with his assistants c. 1438-47 at the Dominican Priory of San Marco. The originality of Fra Angelico's work at the Priory deeply affected his 15th-century admirers and his choice of colourings has deeply affected this needlepoint designer.

I have made this piece into a cushion but it would work equally well as a wall hanging or a photograph album cover. The faces and hands are worked in petit point (see page 115) and are simple to achieve provided you follow the basic instructions.

OPPOSITE: *Angela* after *The Annunciation* by Fra Angelico

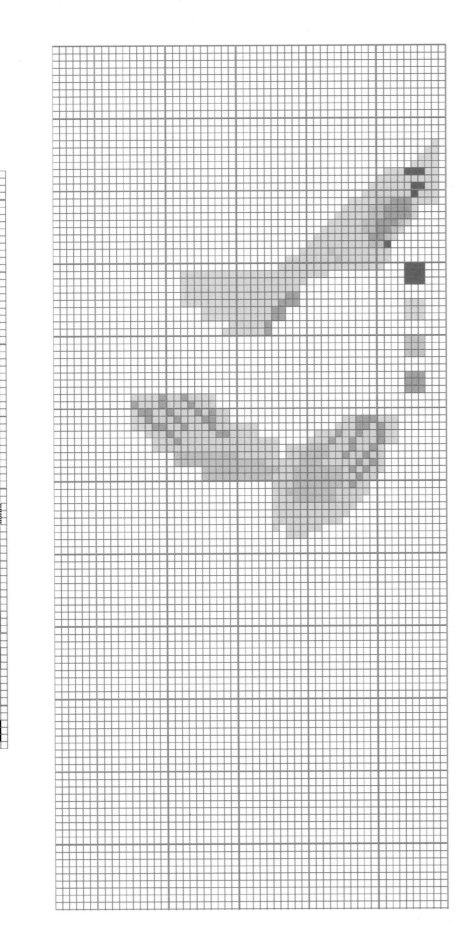

OPPOSITE: Main chart; LEFT: Petit
point chart

YARNS

10m skeins of Anchor Tapisserie Wool in the following colours and quantities:

	Colour	Code	
	Light grey	9764	× 2
	Sea green	8900	× 2
	Old rose	8328	× 1
	Light old rose	8324	× 2
	Mid green	8896	× 2
	Dark gold	8060	× 1
	Light sea green	8892	× 1
	Creamy rose	8322	× 1
	Mid gold	8058	× 1
	Pale maize	8034	× 1
	Light gold	8052	× 2
	Oak brown	9402	× 1
	Dark rose	8330	× 1
	Chocolate	9660	× 2
	Peach	8296	× 1
	Charcoal	9768	× 1

8m skeins of Anchor Stranded Cotton in the following colours and quantities:

	Colour	Code	
	Mid pink	893	× 1
	Pale pink	892	× 1
	Rose	894	× 1
	Grey	235	× 1

MATERIALS

One piece of antique finish, 10 mesh, double canvas measuring 47 × 45.5cm (18½ × 18in). Actual design measures 31.5 × 30.5cm (12½ × 12in).

10m skeins of Anchor Tapisserie Wool in the colours and quantities shown to the left.

8m skeins of Anchor Stranded Cotton in the colours and quantities shown to the right.

Sizes 18 and 22 tapestry needles.

One piece of backing fabric (I have used velvet) measuring 40.5cm (16in) square.

1.5m (5ft) piping cord.

30cm (12in) zip to match backing fabric.

30cm (12in) square cushion pad.

1.5m (5ft) of 2cm (¾in) wide gold, corded braid.

Sewing thread to match backing fabric.

Tools and materials for preparing the canvas (see page 113) and for blocking (see page 116).

WORKING THE DESIGN

Once you have prepared the canvas (see page 114), mount it on a frame (see page 114). Work the petit point detail of the design in half cross stitch, using three strands of cotton (see page 114) and the yarns indicated in the charts on the previous page and the key to the left. Then work the main body of the design using the wool straight from the skein, ie do not split it, and working in half cross stitch throughout.

BLOCKING AND MAKING UP

When the design is complete, block if necessary (see page 116). Once the blocked work is completely dry, make up as a cushion (see page 117).

THE FINAL FEAST

Inspired by *The Last Supper*, Leonardo da Vinci (1452-1519)

The Last Supper by Leonardo da Vinci (1452-1519)

Leonardo was the illegitimate son of a Florentine notary and a peasant girl. Since he is considered the most versatile genius of the Italian Renaissance I hope I will be forgiven for using both *The Last Supper* and *Mona Lisa* as inspiration for my needlepoint designs.

The Last Supper was painted between 1495 and 1497 as a wall painting in the refectory of Sta Maria delle Grazie. Unfortunately, Leonardo found the fresco method of mural work too slow, so he developed his own technique which caused the finished painting to deteriorate rapidly. Although it is still one of the most famous paintings in the world, despite numerous attempts to restore it, it exists in a rather forlorn state.

This design is taken from a William Briggs printed canvas and the faces are worked in petit point (see page 115).

OVERLEAF: *The Final Feast* after *The Last Supper* by Leonardo da Vinci

The Final Feast

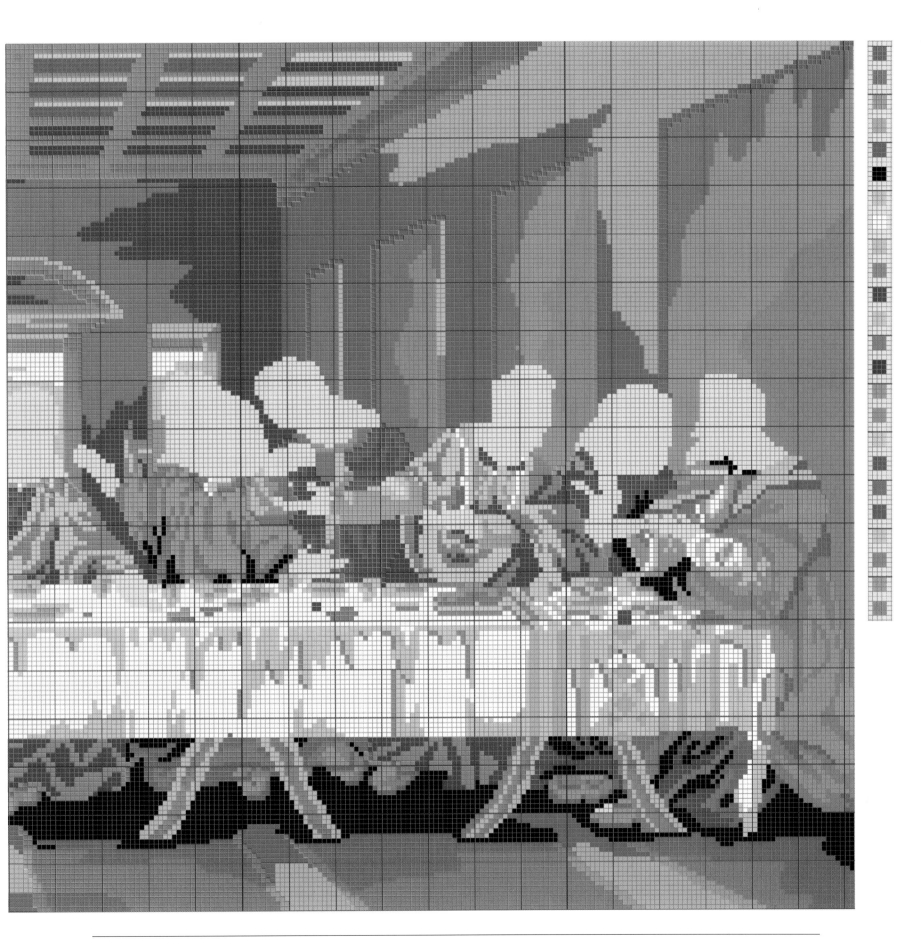

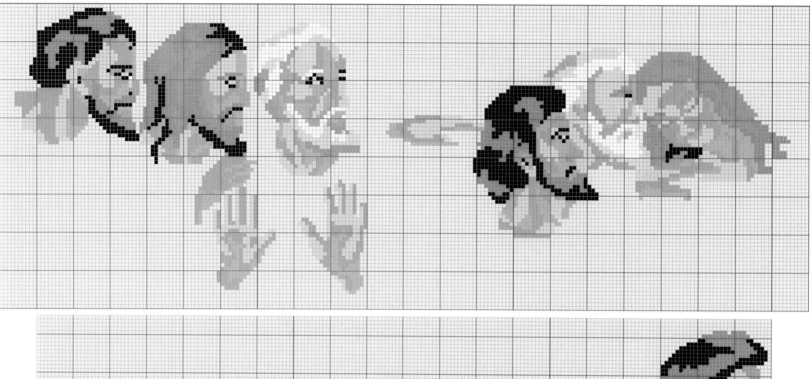

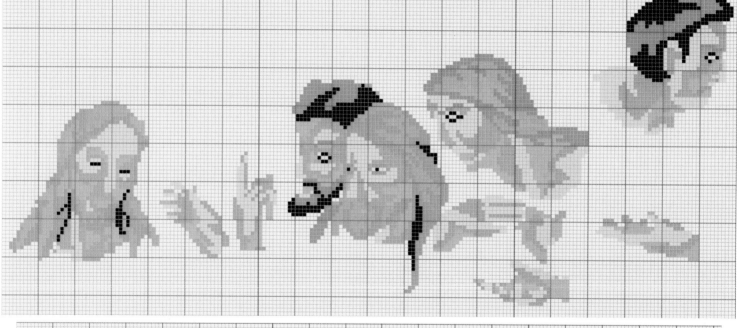

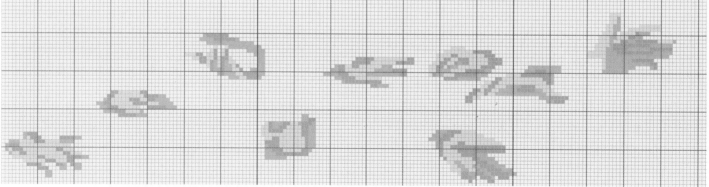

The Final Feast

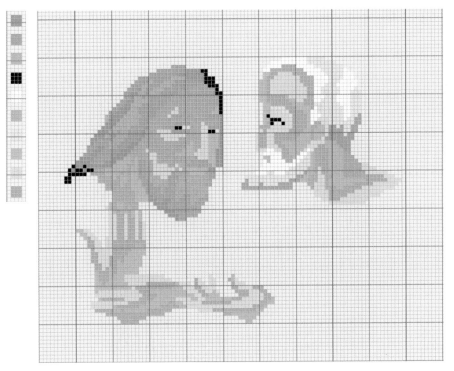

ABOVE & OPPOSITE: The Petit point charts

YARNS

10m skeins of Anchor Tapisserie Wool in the following colours and quantities:

Very dark cinnamon	9394	× 5
Dark cinnamon	9392	× 5
Old gold	8024	× 2
Leaf green	9200	× 5
Bright leaf green	9204	× 4
Chocolate	9648	× 5
Light forest green	9014	× 2
White	8004	× 6
Light cinnamon	9384	× 2
Mid cinnamon	9388	× 5
Rose pink	8404	× 2
Granite	9774	× 2
Dark peacock	8922	× 2
Dark ancient blue	8740	× 6
Salmon pink	8306	× 2
Dark forest green	9018	× 7
Light peacock	8918	× 1
Flame red	8204	× 1
Spruce green	9078	× 2
Light ancient blue	8738	× 1
Light salmon	8302	× 2
Mid peacock	8920	× 4
Pink	8366	× 2
Apricot	9524	× 1

MATERIALS

One piece of antique finish, 10 mesh, double canvas measuring 104 × 61cm (41 × 24in). Actual design measures 91.5 × 45.5cm (36 × 18in).

10m skeins of Anchor Tapisserie Wool in the colours and quantities shown to the left. Tools and materials for preparing the canvas (see page 113), for blocking (see page 116) and for making up (see page 117).

WORKING THE DESIGN

Once you have prepared the canvas (see page 114), mount it on a frame (see page 114). Work the petit point faces using half the thickness of wool (see page 115), then work the main body of the design in half cross stitch. Use the yarns indicated in the charts on pages 18-19 and to the left and above and the key to the left. Use the yarn straight from the skein, ie do not split it.

BLOCKING AND MAKING UP

When the design is complete, block if necessary (see page 116). Once the blocked work is completely dry, mount it on a board (I then chose to mount it on a trunk, see page 116) or frame as required (see page 117).

THAT CERTAIN SMILE

Inspired by *Mona Lisa*, Leonardo da Vinci (1452-1519)

Mona Lisa by Leonardo da Vinci (1452-1519)

Art, back in 1472, was a business and in business you learn to delegate. Such must have been the thinking of Verrocchio back then in Florence. He asked his student Leonardo to help him complete his famous painting *Baptism of Christ*. Reportedly, Leonardo made such a good job of one of the angels, Verrocchio immediately gave up the painting work and left it to the boy.

Taking this as an example, I have decided to chart out da Vinci's most famous work, *Mona Lisa*, for you to stitch. This lady's face is so distinctive that if you produced it in candyfloss pink or neon green the smile would still be recognizable. I must, however, confess to rejuvenating her slightly so if you want her back to her old self you should add some darker shading under the eyes.

I have worked this piece as an oval for a chairback or picture. Half a dozen Mona Lisas sitting around a dining room table could be a sight worth stitching for.

OPPOSITE: *That Certain Smile* after *Mona Lisa* by Leonardo da Vinci

That Certain Smile

YARNS

10m skeins of Anchor Tapisserie
Wool in the following colours
and quantities:

	Cream	9502 × 2
	Green	9180 × 2
	Mid flesh	9506 × 2
	Dark mushroom	9678 × 2
	Flesh	9504 × 1
	Dark green	9182 × 1
	Dark flesh	9508 × 2
	Olive	9328 × 1
	Dark brown	9664 × 6
	Ochre	8048 × 1
	Rose	9620 × 1
	Mushroom	9676 × 2
	Beige	9324 × 1

MATERIALS

One piece of antique finish, 10
mesh, double canvas measuring
61 × 53.5cm (24 × 21in).
Actual design measures 45.5 ×
38cm (18 × 15in).
10m skeins of Anchor Tapisserie
Wool in the colours and
quantities shown above.
Size 18 tapestry needle.
Tools and materials for preparing
the canvas (see page 113), for
blocking (see page 116) and for
making up (see page 117).

WORKING THE DESIGN

Once you have prepared the
canvas (see page 114), mount it
on a frame (see page 114). Work
the design in half cross stitch
throughout using the yarns
indicated in the chart opposite
and the key to left. Use the yarn
straight from the skein, ie do not
split it.

BLOCKING AND MAKING UP

When the design is complete,
block if necessary (see page 116).
Once the blocked work is
completely dry, mount it on your
chairback (see page 116).
Note: If you want to square the
work off, I suggest that you use
the dark brown yarn, 9664, to
give you the most impact.

STONEY SILENCE

Inspired by *Delphic Sibyl*, Michelangelo Buonarroti (1475-1564)

Delphic Sibyl by Michelangelo (1475-1564)

Michelangelo didn't really want the task of painting the ceiling of the Sistine Chapel but he tackled the job of illustrating man's original sin and eventual redemption through Christ with some panache. The work was commissioned in 1508 by Pope Julius II, who anyone would find hard to refuse. But even if the work did result in premature ageing and backache (can you imagine painting this Olympian woman on your ceiling?), it did, after all, make him famous.

Michelangelo was a man of no mean spirit. Some considered his work frightening while others invented a new word for it: 'terribilta'. In fact, he was one of the few artists to become a myth in his own lifetime. For such a clever man, you would have thought he might have looked after himself better than he did. He didn't change his clothes very often and when he eventually took his breeches off it was suggested that his skin peeled off with them.

To me, the image of the *Delphic Sibyl* epitomizes the feminist movement in full swing. The needlepoint comprises of big blocks of colour so, while it is a relatively large piece, it's a simple one for a beginner.

OVERLEAF: *Stoney Silence* after *Delphic Sibyl* by Michelangelo

YARNS

10m skeins of Anchor Tapisserie Wool in the following colours and quantities.

Colour	Code	Qty
Rose	9620	× 1
Mid flesh	9616	× 5
Rust	9560	× 2
Slate	8720	× 3
Pale flesh	9592	× 2
Mid green	9174	× 1
Dark blue	8630	× 2
Grey	8716	× 2
Stone	9772	× 2
White	8002	× 3
Mid blue	8628	× 2
Dark green	9178	× 3
Dark flesh	9618	× 4
Silver	9774	× 3
Grey	9776	× 4
Light green	9212	× 2
Copper	9564	× 4
Olive	8048	× 1
Gold	8044	× 1

MATERIALS

One piece of antique finish, 10 mesh, double canvas measuring 73.5 × 68.5cm (29 × 27in). Actual design measures 63.5 × 58.5cm (25 × 23 in).
10m skeins of Anchor Tapisserie Wool in the colours and quantities shown to the left.
Size 18 tapestry needle.
Tools and materials for preparing the canvas (see page 113), for blocking (see page 116) and for making up (see page 117).

WORKING THE DESIGN

Once you have prepared the canvas (see page 114), mount it on a frame (see page 114). Work the design in half cross stitch throughout using the yarns indicated in the chart on page 27 and the key to the left. Use the yarn straight from the skein, ie do not split it.

BLOCKING AND MAKING UP

When the design is complete, block if necessary (see page 116). Once the blocked work is completely dry, mount it on a board (I then chose to mount it on a firescreen, see page 116) or frame as required (see page 114).

CHILD ANGELS

Inspired by a detail from *The Sistine Madonna*, Raphael (1483-1520)

Detail from *The Sistine Madonna* by Raphael (1483-1520)

Raffaello Sanzio (Raphael to you), was an Italian artist and architect of the High Renaissance School. Influenced strongly by Michelangelo and Leonardo, Raphael was a gentle soul whose humanity showed strongly through his work. His influence in this book is particularly appropriate since it was Raphael who was responsible for producing the cartoons for the tapestries in the Sistine Chapel. This particular design is inspired by a small image taken from his greatest work, *The Sistine Madonna* painted in 1512. The expressions on the faces of the child angels make them strangely contemporary and irresistible for my purposes. But these two tousle-haired cherubs have a problem: how is the one on the left going to fly when he has only one wing?

The design measures 30.5cm × 40.5cm (12 × 16in) and has here been made up into this exquisite cushion (see page 117 for making instructions) but it could just as easily be mounted and made into a framed picture or used as a stool cover.

YARNS

10m skeins of Anchor Tapisserie
Wool in the following colours
and quantities:

▦	Dark grey	9768 × 2
▦	Donkey	9680 × 2
▦	Beige	9676 × 2
▦	Dark flesh	9508 × 2
▦	Mid flesh	9506 × 1
▦	Light flesh	9504 × 1
▦	Yellow	8058 × 2
▦	Pale yellow	8038 × 3
☐	White	8002 × 1
▦	Mulberry	8420 × 1
▦	Orange	8140 × 1
▦	Red	8200 × 1
▦	Silver	9776 × 1
▦	Copper	9494 × 1
▦	Mid grey	9764 × 1
▦	Chocolate	9646 × 1
■	Black	9800 × 2
▦	Cream	9502 × 1

MATERIALS

One piece of antique finish, 10
mesh, double canvas measuring
51 × 40.5cm (20 × 16in).
Actual design measures 40.5 ×
30.5cm (16 × 12in).
10m skeins of Anchor Tapisserie
Wool in the colours and
quantities shown to the left.
Size 18 tapestry needle.
One piece of backing fabric (I
have used velvet) measuring 50
× 120cm (18 × 48in).
30cm (12in) zip to match
backing fabric.
2.2m (7ft) piping cord.
58.5 × 48cm (23 × 19in)
cushion pad.
Sewing thread to match backing
fabric.
Tools and materials for preparing
the canvas (see page 113), for
blocking (see page 116) and for
making up (see page 117).

WORKING THE DESIGN

Once you have prepared the
canvas (see page 114), mount it
on a frame (see page 114). Work
the design in half cross stitch
throughout using the yarns
indicated in the chart on the
previous page and the key to the
left. Use the yarn straight from
the skein, ie do not split it.

BLOCKING AND MAKING UP

When the design is complete,
block if necessary (see page 116).
Once the blocked work is
completely dry, make up as a
cushion (see page 117).

OPPOSITE: *Child Angels* after a detail
from *The Sistine Madonna* by Raphael

LULLABY
Inspired by *Angel Playing the Lute*, Giovanni Battista Rosso Fiorentino (1494-1540)

Angel Playing the Lute by Rosso (1494-1540)

Rosso was a Florentine, an individualist, and one of the leading figures in the development of Mannerism, a term derived from the Italian *Maniera* which translates to style or stylishness. This term is used particularly to describe Italian works that were produced between the High Renaissance and the Baroque, from 1520 to 1600.

Rosso's style, or work, and choice of subject varied greatly and in 1530 he was invited to France by Francis I. Rosso then worked on the decoration of the royal palace at Fontainebleau where his principal work was the Gallery of Francis I. Many engravings were produced from his designs and this angel playing the lute is my personal favourite.

OPPOSITE: *Lullaby* after *Angel Playing the Lute* by Rosso

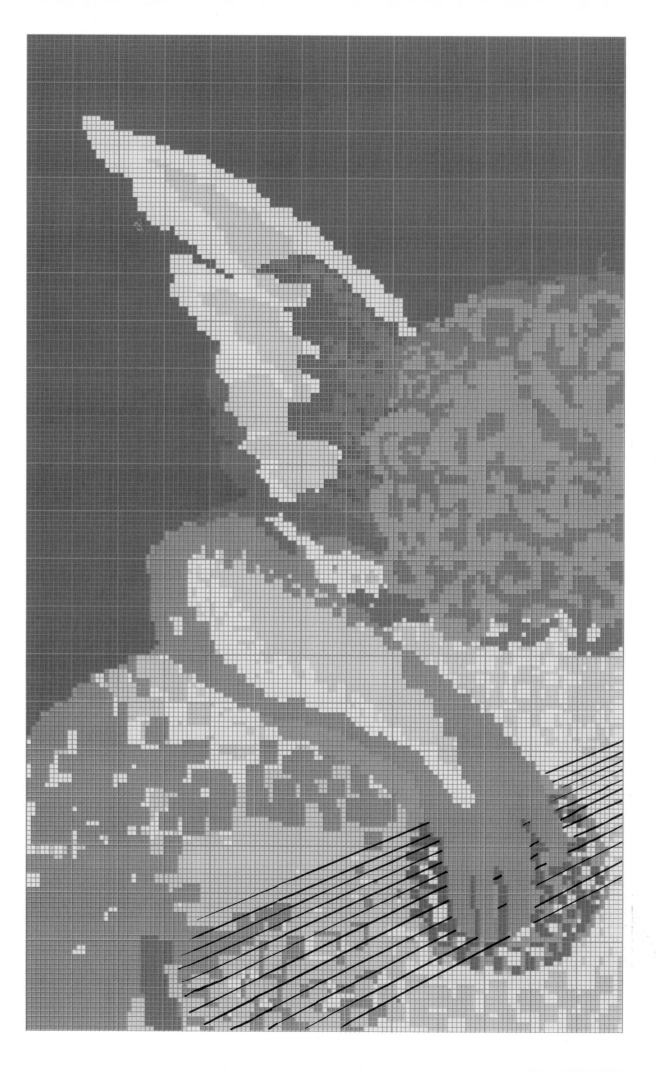

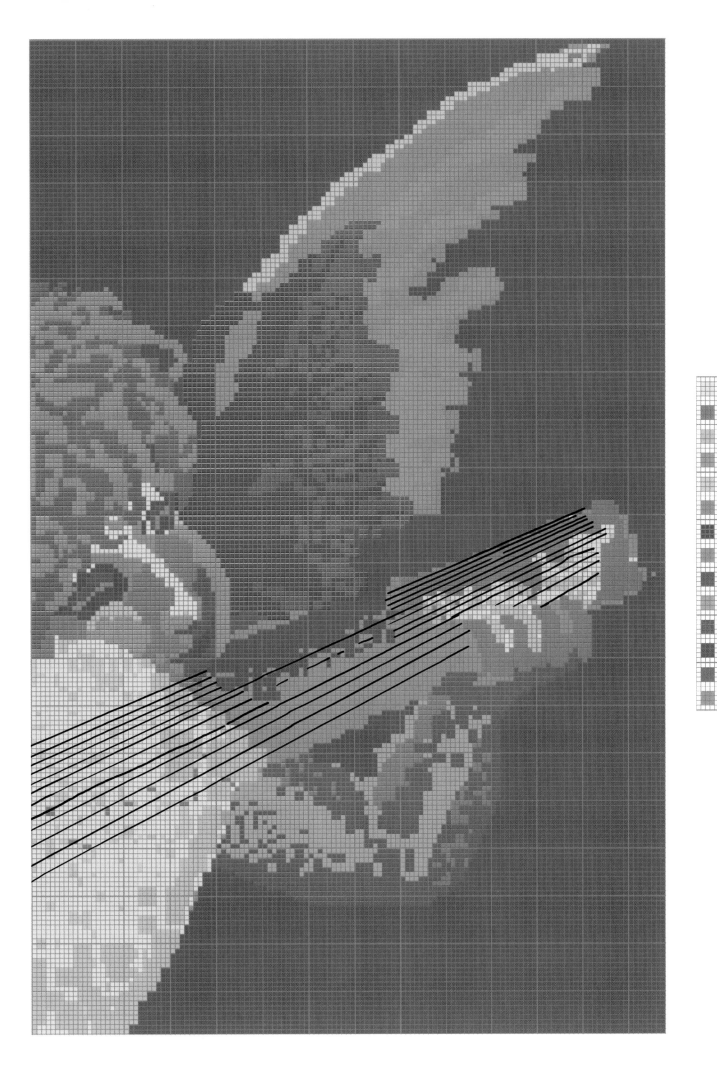

39

YARNS

8m skeins of Anchor Stranded Cotton in the following colours and quantities:

	Colour		
	Cream	366	× 2
	Copper	369	× 3
	Honey	363	× 3
	Pale green	843	× 1
	Pale gold	887	× 2
	Coffee	373	× 2
	Red	335	× 1
	Pink	895	× 1
	Dark coffee	903	× 1
	Mushroom	233	× 1
	Dark red	13	× 1
	Dark green	862	× 9
	Rust	884	× 1
	Gold	307	× 2

In addition, a skein of black (403) is required for the lute strings.

MATERIALS

One piece of antique finish, 18 mesh, single canvas measuring 40.5 × 48.5cm (16 × 19in). Actual design measures 29.5 × 37.5cm (11⁶⁄₁₀ × 14⁸⁄₁₀in). 8m skeins of Anchor Stranded Cotton in the colours and quantities shown to the left. Size 22 tapestry needle. Tools and materials for preparing the canvas (see page 113), for blocking (see page 116) and for making up (see page 117).

WORKING THE DESIGN

Once you have prepared the canvas (see page 114), mount it on a framed (see page 114). Work the design in half cross stitch throughout using the yarns indicated in the chart on the previous page and the key to the left. Use four strands of cotton. When the design is complete add the strings of the lute in back stitch using black, 403.

BLOCKING AND MAKING UP

When the design is complete, block if necessary (see page 116). Once the blocked work is completely dry, mount it on a board (I then chose to mount it on a wall cupboard, see page 116) or frame as required (see page 117).

MAN FOR ALL SEASONS

Inspired by *The Laughing Cavalier*, Frans Hals (1581/5-1666)

The Laughing Cavalier by Frans Hals (1581/5-1666)

Although he painted with dashing bravado, the Dutch artist Hals had plenty of problems in his private life. Constantly in financial trouble, Hals married twice and had ten children. He was rumoured to be a heavy drinker and his second wife was frequently in trouble for public brawling.

It was not until the second half of the 19th century that Hals' genius was recognized and rewarded. Lord Herford bought *The Laughing Cavalier* for 51,000 francs which was then an enormous sum of money. This immediately made his work sought after, particularly among the Americans who have many of Hals' portraits in their collections.

This design was produced by William Briggs Ltd, and sold as a very popular painted canvas for a number of years.

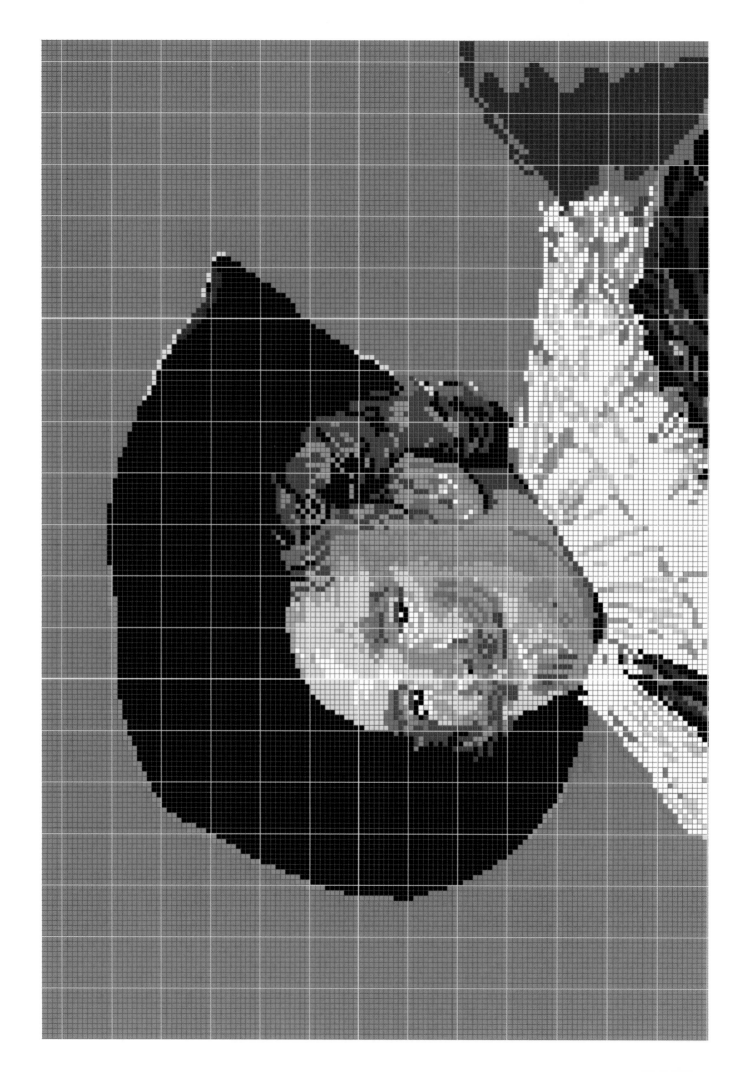

43

YARNS

10m skeins of Anchor Tapisserie
Wool in the following colours
and quantities:

■	Black	9800 ×	11
	Mid chestnut	9560 ×	2
	Dark terracotta	8264 ×	1
▢	Ecru	8006 ×	5
	Pale coffee	9386 ×	1
	Mid nutmeg	9448 ×	1
	Yellow	8120 ×	2
	Light yellow	8132 ×	1
	Dark coffee	9640 ×	1
	Charcoal	9678 ×	2
	Granite	9776 ×	10
■	Mid grey	9766 ×	4
	Pale grey	9786 ×	1
	Old rose	8326 ×	1
	Olive	9314 ×	1
	Light nutmeg	9442 ×	1
	Light mahogany	9596 ×	1
	Brown	9642 ×	1
	Pale mink	9672 ×	2
	Coffee	9638 ×	1

MATERIALS

One piece of antique finish, 10
mesh, double canvas measuring
76 × 58.5cm (30 × 23in).
Actual design measures 66 ×
48cm (26 × 19in).
10m skeins of Anchor Tapisserie
Wool in the colours and
quantities shown to the left.
Size 18 tapestry needle.
Tools and materials for preparing
the canvas (see page 113), for
blocking (see page 116) and for
making up (see page 117).

WORKING THE DESIGN

Once you have prepared the
canvas (see page 114), mount it
on a frame (see page 114). Work
the design in half cross stitch
throughout using the yarns
indicated in the chart on the
previous pages and the key to the
left. Use the yarn straight from
the skein, ie do not split it.

BLOCKING AND MAKING UP

When the design is complete,
block if necessary (see page 116).
Once the blocked work is
completely dry, mount it on a
board and the needlepoint will be
ready to frame as required (see
page 117).

Man for All Seasons after *The
Laughing Cavalier* by Frans Hals

HOME SWEET HOME

Inspired by *Lady and Gentleman at the Virginals*, Johannes Vermeer (1632-75)

Lady and Gentleman at the Virginals by Johannes Vermeer (1632-75)

Vermeer was a man fascinated by domestic order. His characters appear to live in a world of tranquil pastimes such as reading, music and lacemaking. A great master of the Dutch School he managed to keep his wife and 11 children on the proceeds of the sale of just 30-40 paintings. Compared to his contemporaries Rembrandt and Hals, this could definitely be considered unprolific. To supplement his income, he wheeled and dealed in art and relied in some measure on his wealthy mother-in-law and his patron, Pieter van Ruijven, a Delft collector.

The painting that that has inspired this needlepoint is part of the Royal Collection of HM Queen Elizabeth II of England and resides at St James's Palace, London. No needlework book would be complete without a Home Sweet Home picture and who better to turn to than Vermeer for the project?

OPPOSITE: *Home Sweet Home* after *Lady and Gentleman at the Virginals* by Johannes Vermeer

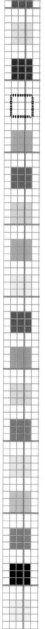

49

YARNS

10m skeins of Anchor Tapisserie Wool in the following colours and quantities:

	Colour		
	Grey green	9068	× 2
	Brown	9662	× 2
	Silver	9784	× 1
	Chocolate	9664	× 2
	White	8000	× 1
	Gold	8024	× 1
	Olive	9310	× 1
	Old gold	8042	× 1
	Green/grey	9054	× 1
	Butter	8054	× 1
	Dark red	8312	× 2
	Blue	8630	× 1
	Light blue	8628	× 1
	Charcoal	9798	× 4
	Pink	9614	× 1
	Dark pink	9618	× 1
	Red	8238	× 1
	Black	9800	× 2
	Cream	9402	× 1

MATERIALS

One piece of antique finish, 12 mesh, double canvas measuring 48 × 39.5cm (19 × 15½in). Actual design measures 38 × 28cm (15 × 11in).

10m skeins of Anchor Tapisserie Wool in the colours and quantities shown to the left.

Size 18 tapestry needle.

Tools and materials for preparing the canvas (see page 113), for blocking (see page 116) and for making up (see page 117).

WORKING THE DESIGN

Once you have prepared the canvas (see page 114), mount it on a frame (see page 114). Work the design in half cross stitch throughout using the yarns indicated in the chart on the previous page and the key to the left. Use the yarn straight from the skein, ie do not split it.

BLOCKING AND MAKING UP

When the design is complete, block if necessary (see page 116). Once the blocked work is completely dry, mount it on a board (I then chose to mount it on a writing box, see page 116) or frame as required (see page 117).

FLORAL TRIBUTE

Inspired by *Floral Composition*, Gerard van Spaendonck (1746-1822)

The stitched picture of *Floral Composition* by Gerard van Spaendonck (1746-1822)

Gerard and his brother Cornelius van Spaendonck were both highly respected painters of flowers, although Cornelius used his talent to decorate porcelain at the Sevres Factory. Born in Tilburgh in Holland, Gerard studied under Herreyns at Antwerp and at the age of 24 years moved to Paris where he specialized in painting miniatures, and fruit and flowers. His work was very popular and sold extremely well.

In 1793, van Spaendonck lectured at the Jardin des Plantes and we are told through his work *Fleurs Dessinées d'après Nature* that he was a member of the National Institute and Professor cum Administrator of the Natural History Museum in Paris. He has a fruit and flower painting in the Louvre which was in the collection of Louis XVI.

This design is produced as a printed canvas by Royal Paris in France, I have simply charted their interpretation.

53

YARNS

10m skeins of Anchor Tapisserie Wool in the following colours and quantities:

	Colour	Number		Qty
	Chocolate	9666	×	13
	Cinnamon	9390	×	3
	Grass green	9162	×	5
	Apple green	9100	×	3
	Dark olive	9178	×	3
	Brown olive	9306	×	2
	Leaf green	9208	×	17
	White	8000	×	7
	Brick	9612	×	2
	Magenta	8484	×	2
	Raspberry	8416	×	2
	Rose pink	8400	×	2
	Flame red	8204	×	1
	Maize	8042	×	3
	Old gold	8016	×	2
	Periwinkle	8610	×	2
	Pale blue	8604	×	2
	Pale grey	8712	×	2
	Cornflower	8686	×	2
	Granite	9772	×	5
	Light olive	9174	×	3
	Nutmeg	9452	×	4

OPPOSITE: *Floral Tribute* after *Floral Composition* by Gerard van Spaendonck

MATERIALS

One piece of antique finish, 10 mesh, double canvas measuring 75 × 90cm (29½ × 35½in). Actual design measures 66 × 81cm (26 × 32in).

10m skeins of Anchor Tapisserie Wool in the colours and quantities shown to the left.

Size 18 tapestry needle.

Tools and materials for preparing the canvas (see page 113), for blocking (see page 116) and for making up (see page 117).

WORKING THE DESIGN

Once you have prepared the canvas (see page 114), mount it on a frame (see page 114). Work the design in half cross stitch throughout using the yarns indicated in the chart on the previous page and the key to the left. Use the yarn straight from the skein, ie do not split it.

BLOCKING AND MAKING UP

When the design is complete, block if necessary (see page 116). Once the blocked work is completely dry, mount it on a board and the needlepoint will be ready to frame as required (see page 117).

RED VELVET

Inspired by *Don Manuel Osorio de Zuniga*, Francisco de Goya (1746-1828)

Don Manuel Osorio de Zuniga by Franciso de Goya (1746-1828)

Goya was probably the most original European artist of his time. Born in Spain he married and settled in Madrid and from 1775 to 1792 he produced 63 cartoons for the royal tapestry factory. He went on to become a celebrated portrait painter until he was struck by a mysterious illness that left him deaf. From this time the nature of his work changed and he began to produce compositions of bizarre and menacing images. His work was often satirical and had both a humorous and nightmarish element. In later years, Goya moved to Bordeaux and took up the medium of lithography.

For those who enjoy fine work, you may like to reproduce this chart on silk gauze using fine stranded cotton. As well as making a fine portrait for the dining room, it is also an excellent subject for a miniature.

OPPOSITE: *Red Velvet* after *Don Manuel Osorio de Zuniga* by Francisco de Goya

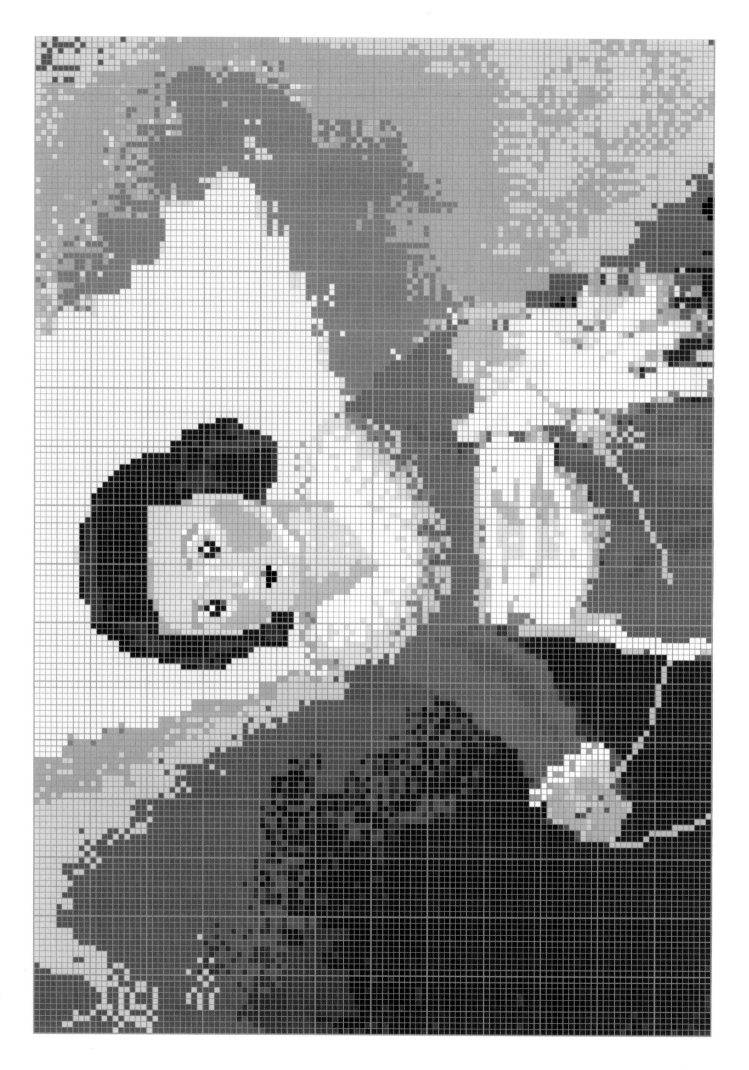

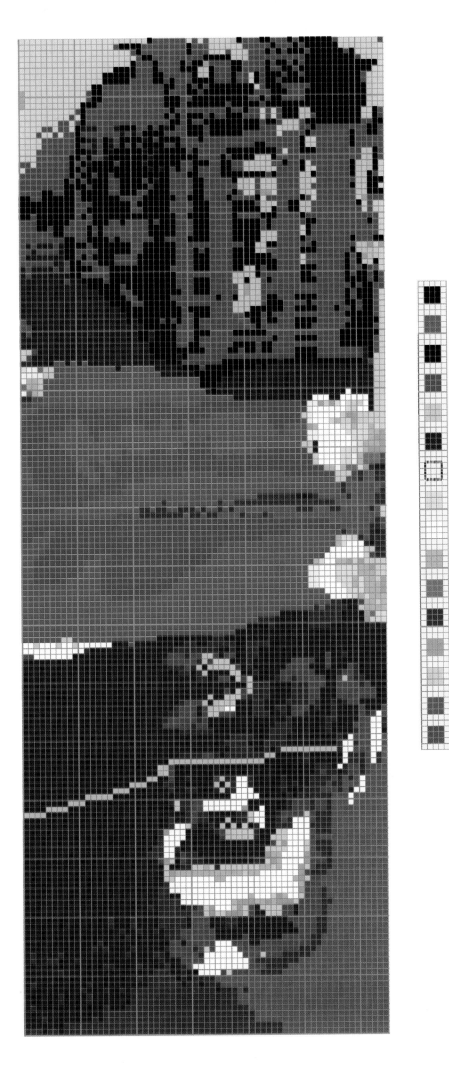

59

YARNS

10m skeins of Anchor Tapisserie Wool in the following colours and quantities:

	Colour	Code	Qty
▦	Priest grey	9764	× 3
▦	Cherry red	8218	× 1
	Light mink	9672	× 2
	Dark mink	9676	× 2
▦	Grey	9796	× 2
	Mink	9678	× 2
	Mid flesh	9506	× 2
	White	8000	× 1
	Pale flesh	9502	× 1
▢	Cream	9382	× 2
▦	Dark grey	9768	× 4
	Yellow	8136	× 1
▦	Dark cherry red	8220	× 1
▦	Black	9800	× 2
	Chestnut	9566	× 2
▦	Terracotta	8260	× 1

MATERIALS

One piece of antique finish, 12 mesh, single canvas measuring 51 × 45.5cm (20 × 18in). Actual design measures 39.5 × 35.5cm (15½ × 14in).

10m skeins of Anchor Tapisserie Wool in the colours and quantities shown to the left.

Size 18 tapestry needle.

Tools and materials for preparing the canvas (see page 113), for blocking (see page 116) and for making up (see page 117).

WORKING THE DESIGN

Once you have prepared the canvas (see page 114), mount it on a frame (see page 114). Work the design in half cross stitch throughout using the yarns indicated in the chart on the previous page and the key to the left. Use the yarn straight from the skein, ie do not split it.

BLOCKING AND MAKING UP

When the design is complete, block if necessary (see page 116). Once the blocked work is completely dry, mount it on a board and the needlepoint will be ready to frame as required (see page 117).

COUNTRY DIARY

Inspired by *Flatford Mill*, John Constable (1776-1837)

Detail from *Flatford Mill* by John Constable (1776-1837)

Constable had a profound love of the countryside and along with Turner is
considered one of the greatest painters of British landscapes. His finest works were
of places that he lived in Suffolk and Hampstead and his interpretation of the scenes
there stem from his belief that "no two days are alike nor even two hours; neither
were there ever two leaves of a tree alike since the creation of the world". His
approach to painting was to make full-size oil sketches (some praised more
than the finished work for their freshness) on site which he would then complete
in his studio. His work had a great influence on the Romantics and also
on the Impressionists.

LEFT: *Country Diary* after *Flatford Mill* by John Constable

65

YARNS

10m skeins of Anchor Tapisserie Wool in the following colours and quantities:

▦	Nutmeg	9448	× 2
▦	Dark cinnamon	9394	× 4
▦	Sand	9524	× 1
▦	Brown olive	9314	× 6
▦	Chestnut	9560	× 1
▦	Forest green	9018	× 2
▦	White	8006	× 3
▦	Chocolate	9666	× 4
▦	Khaki	9324	× 2
▦	Heraldic gold	9290	× 3
▦	Light cinnamon	9388	× 3
▦	Dark blue	8738	× 1
▦	Olive green	9174	× 4
▦	Moss green	9212	× 3
▦	Beige brown	9640	× 2
▦	China blue	8624	× 3
▦	Dove grey	8892	× 4
▦	Yellow	8116	× 1
▦	Grey	8712	× 4
▦	Light blue	8734	× 2

MATERIALS

One piece of antique finish, 10 mesh, double canvas measuring 66 × 56cm (26 × 22in). Actual design measures 56 × 46cm (22 × 18in).

10m skeins of Anchor Tapisserie Wool in the colours and quantities shown to the left.

Size 18 tapestry needle.

Tools and materials for preparing the canvas (see page 113), for blocking (see page 116) and for making up (see page 117).

WORKING THE DESIGN

Once you have prepared the canvas (see page 114), mount it on a frame (see page 114). Work the design in half cross stitch throughout using the yarns indicated in the chart on the previous page and the key to the left. Use the yarn straight from the skein, ie do not split it.

BLOCKING AND MAKING UP

When the design is complete, block if necessary (see page 116). Once the blocked work is completely dry, mount it on a board and the needlepoint will be ready to frame as required (see page 117).

GREEN SLEEVES

Inspired by *Veronica Veronese*, Dante Gabriel Rossetti (1828-82)

Veronica Veronesse by Dante Gabriel Rossetti (1828-82)

Of all the Pre-Raphaelite ladies, this has to be my favourite. The portrait is of Alexa Wilding who appears in many of Rossetti's works and has the features and colouring strongly associated with this era.

The Pre-Raphaelite movement was a little tired by the time Rossetti, William Morris and Edward Burne-Jones came on the scene. But the arrival of these masters provided a breath of fresh air and their paintings overspilled into decorative arts, furnishings and even literature.

Rossetti was an eccentric Bohemian who shared his home with numerous strange creatures such as wombats and wallabies. In later years he suffered from a persecution complex and even attempted suicide although on his better days he was a fascinating, witty man and a great admirer of female beauty.

LEFT: *Green Sleeves* after *Veronica Veronese* by Dante Gabriel Rossetti

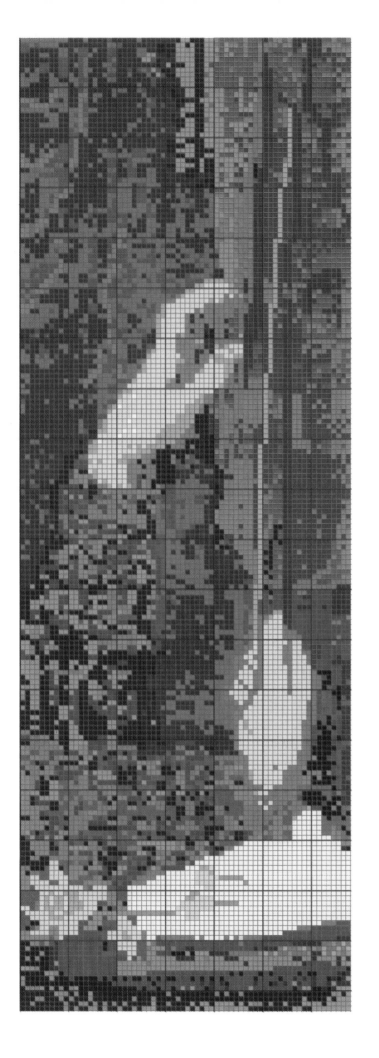

YARNS

10m skeins of Anchor Tapisserie Wool in the following colours and quantities:

	Colour	Code	Qty
	Dark green	9008	× 1
	Moss green	9198	× 2
	Light flesh	9502	× 3
	Coffee	9490	× 1
	Grey/green	9206	× 5
	Green	9006	× 2
	Beige	9486	× 1
	Bright green	9202	× 3
	Dark green	9082	× 3
	Aqua	9004	× 3
	Brown	9292	× 2
	Flesh	9504	× 2
	Grey	9068	× 2
	Dark rust	9540	× 2
	Olive gold	9288	× 4
	Mid orange	9536	× 1
	Chestnut	9496	× 1
	Dark ochre	9406	× 1
	Yellow	8096	× 1
	Dark yellow	8098	× 1
	Orange	9538	× 2
	Milky coffee	9404	× 1
	Lime	9212	× 1

MATERIALS

One piece of antique finish, 10 mesh, double canvas measuring 66 × 60cm (26 × 23½in). Actual design measures 53.5 × 49.5cm (21 × 19½in).
10m skeins of Anchor Tapisserie Wool in the colours and quantities shown to the left.
Size 18 tapestry needle.
One piece of backing fabric (I have used velvet) measuring 1m × 120cm (36 × 48in).
46cm (18in) zip to match backing fabric.
51 × 48cm (20 × 19in) cushion pad.
Sewing thread to match backing fabric.
Tools and materials for preparing the canvas (see page 113) and for blocking (see page 116).

WORKING THE DESIGN

Once you have prepared the canvas (see page 114), mount it on a frame (see page 114). Work the design in half cross stitch throughout using the yarns indicated in the chart on the previous page and the key to the left. Use the yarn straight from the skein, ie do not split it.

BLOCKING AND MAKING UP

When the design is complete, block if necessary (see page 116). Once the blocked work is completely dry, make up as a cushion (see page 117) or mount it on a board and frame as required (see page 117).

SOAP OPERA

Inspired by *Bubbles*, Sir John Everett Millais (1829-96)

Bubbles by Sir John Everett Millais (1829-96)

An immediate contemporary of Lord Leighton, Millais was a naturally gifted child prodigy who became a student at the Royal Academy, London when he was only 11 years old. He was one of the founders of the Pre-Raphaelite Brotherhood although from 1850 his subject matter changed from serious to sentimental scenes.

He was also a book illustrator and achieved notable success with his illustrations for Anthony Trollope's works. Many considered his later work to be a little too commercially oriented although Millais vehemently denied this, writing that he "never consciously placed an idle touch upon canvas". Intentionally or not, his portrait of *Bubbles*, which inspired this William Briggs needlepoint, certainly served one company well. It is owned by A & F Pears Ltd, celebrated for their mild and gentle soap.

YARNS

10m skeins of Anchor Tapisserie Wool in the following colours and quantities:

	Colour	Code	
	Beige brown	9646	× 4
	Leaf green	9204	× 1
	Cinnamon	9430	× 6
	Brown olive	9312	× 3
	Spruce	9022	× 1
	Dark spruce	9208	× 1
	Olive	9174	× 1
	Yellow	8016	× 1
	Ecru	8006	× 1
	Chestnut	9560	× 1
	Bronze flesh	9442	× 1
	Snuff	9592	× 1
	Chocolate	9666	× 5
	Sage	9172	× 1
	Tapestry green	9324	× 1
	Sea green	8876	× 1
	Autumn gold	8132	× 1
	Nutmeg	9448	× 1

MATERIALS

One piece of antique finish, 10 mesh, double canvas measuring 45.5 × 53.5cm (18 × 21in). Actual design measures 35.5 × 43cm (14 × 17in).

10m skeins of Anchor Tapisserie Wool in the colours and quantities shown to the left. Sizes 18 and 22 tapestry needles. Tools and materials for preparing the canvas (see page 113), for blocking (see page 116) and for making up (see page 117).

WORKING THE DESIGN

Once you have prepared the canvas (see page 114), mount it on a frame (see page 114). Work the petit point face using half the thickness of wool (see page 115), then work the main body of the design in half cross stitch throughout. Use the yarns indicated in the charts overleaf and the key to the left. Use the yarn straight from the skein, ie do not split it.

BLOCKING AND MAKING UP

When the design is complete, block if necessary (see page 116). Once the blocked work is completely dry, mount it on a board and the needlepoint will be ready to frame as required (see page 117).

OPPOSITE: *Soap Opera* after *Bubbles* by Sir John Everett Millais

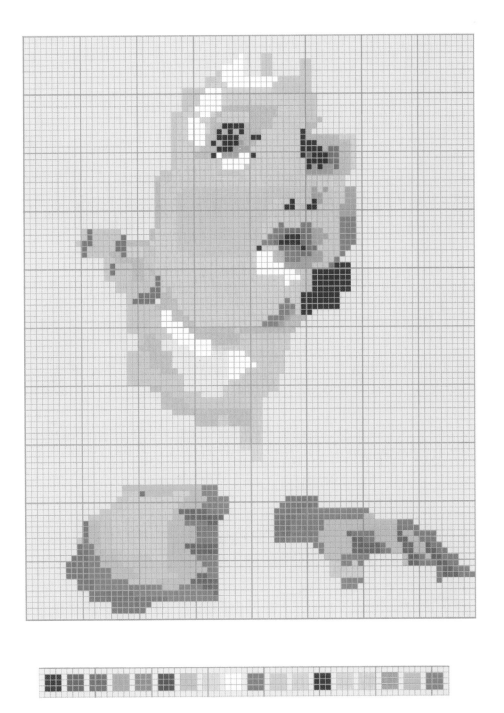

LEFT: Main chart; ABOVE: Petit point chart

LADY IN RED

Inspired by *Flaming June*, Frederic (Lord) Leighton (1830-96)

Flaming June by Frederic Leighton (1830-96)

While many of the artists featured in this book lived tortured lives and died in abject poverty, Leighton lived and died in style. In 1878 he was made president of the Royal Academy, in 1886 a Baronet, and on the day before his death he was made a Lord.

Flaming June was exhibited at the Royal Academy summer exhibition of 1895. Leighton commented that "the design was not a deliberate one, but was suggested by a chance attitude of a weary model who had a particularly supple figure." The colours send out an extraordinary glow which reflects on the skin tones and the background.

OPPOSITE: Detail from *Lady in Red*

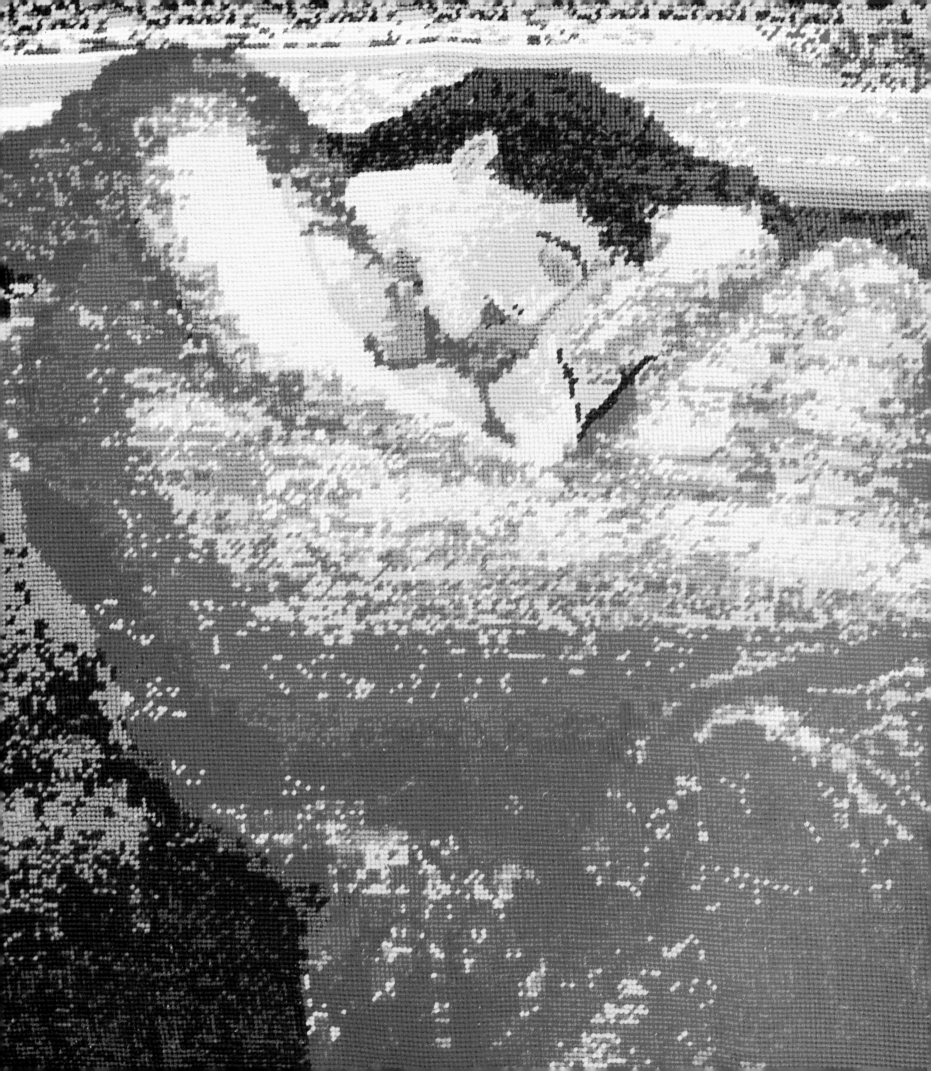

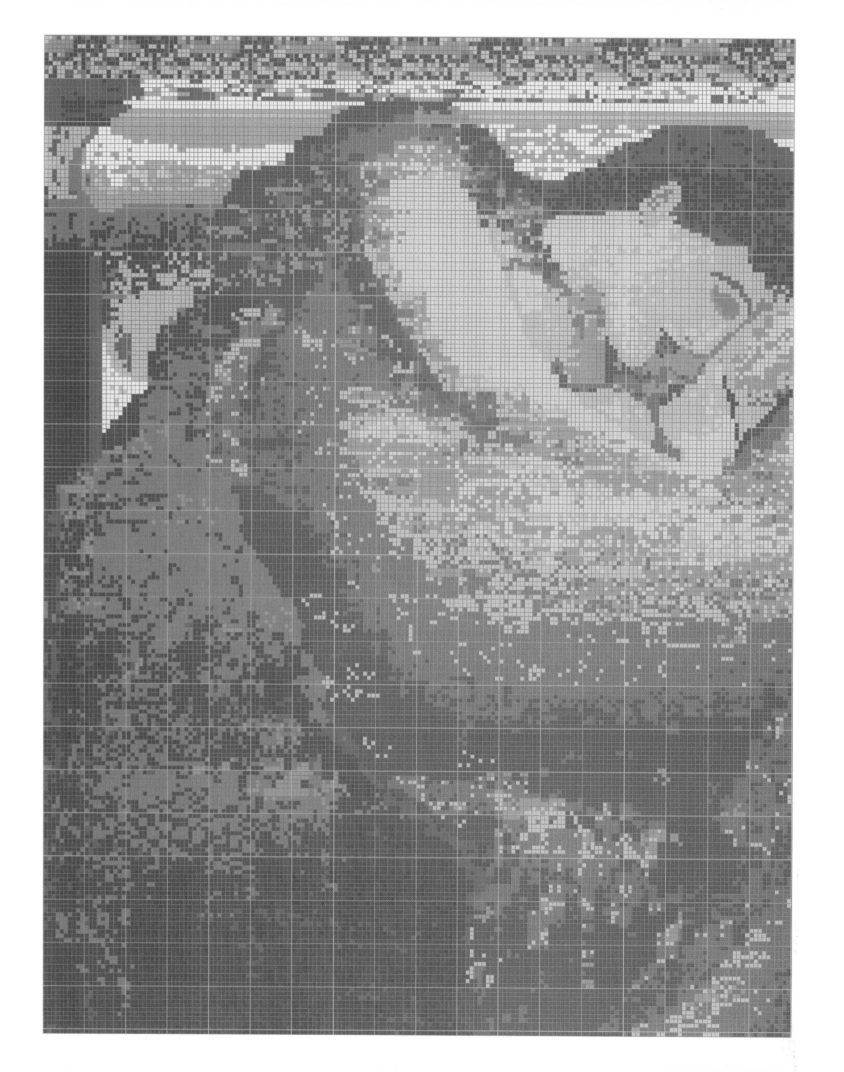

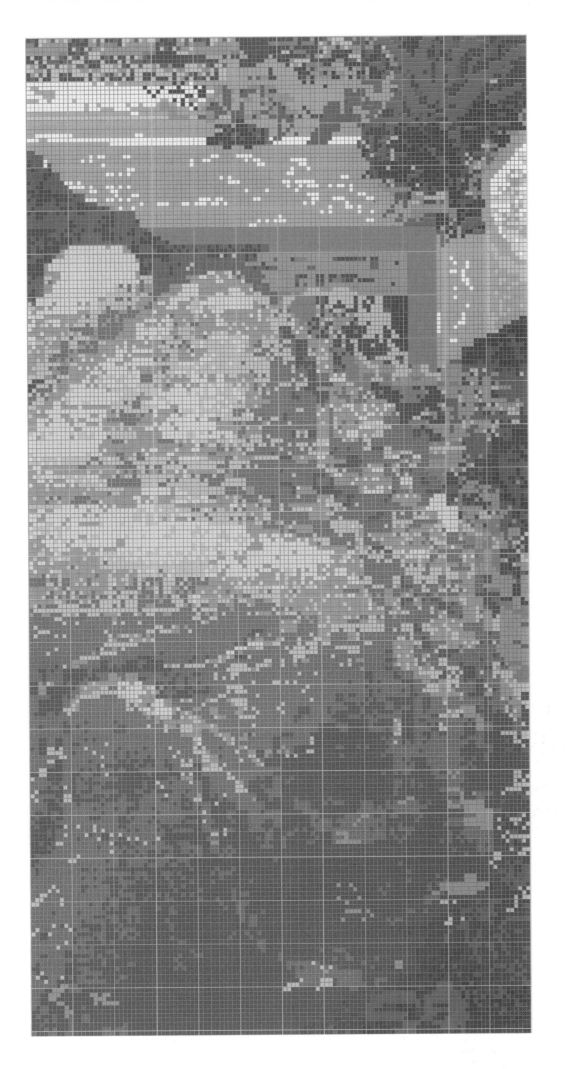

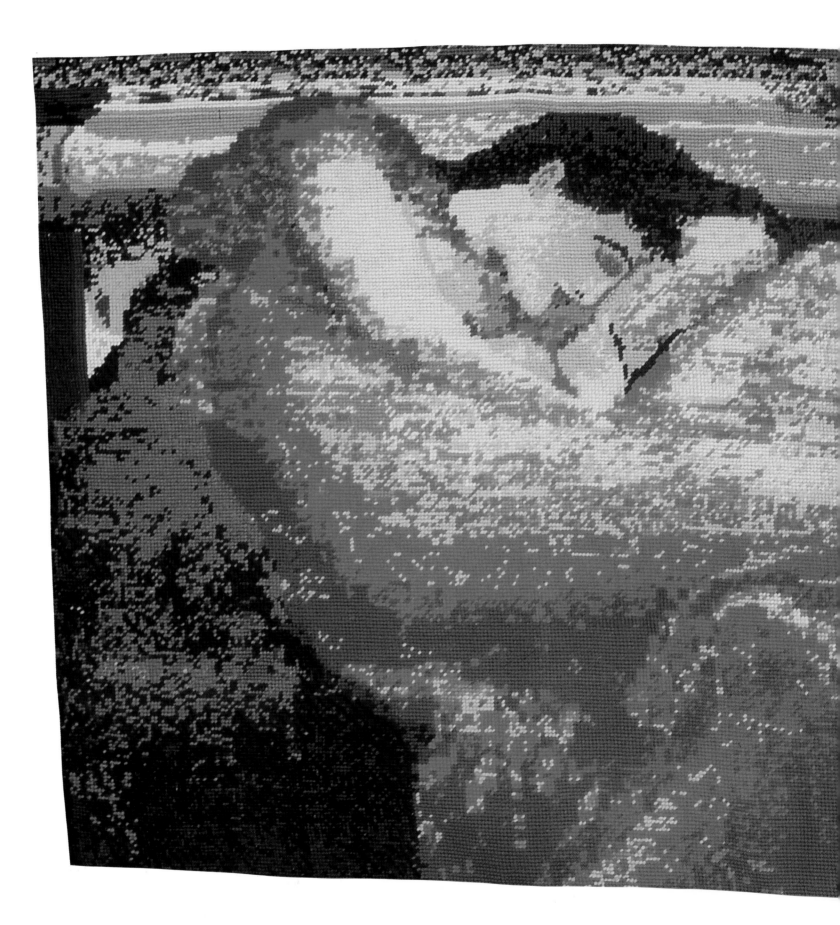

Lady in Red

YARNS

10m skeins of Anchor Tapisserie Wool in the following colours and quantities:

▨	Mahogany	9602 ×	4
▨	Pale yellow	8132 ×	6
▨	Beige	9658 ×	2
▨	Toffee	8106 ×	3
▨	Apricot	8138 ×	10
▨	Mustard	8102 ×	4
▨	Beige gold	8042 ×	6
▨	Red brown	9450 ×	4
▨	Dark orange	8168 ×	12
▨	Rust	8162 ×	12
▨	Orange	8166 ×	7
▢	Cream	8038 ×	3
▨	Green	9022 ×	1
▨	Rusty red	8216 ×	1

MATERIALS

One piece of antique finish, 10 mesh, double canvas measuring 73.5 × 91.5cm (29 × 36in). Actual design measures 57 × 75cm (22½ × 29½in).
10m skeins of Anchor Tapisserie Wool in the colours and quantities shown above.
Size 18 tapestry needle.
One piece of backing fabric (I have used velvet) measuring 125 × 120cm (54 × 48in).
61cm (24in) zip to match backing fabric.
3.5m (4yd) piping cord.

Three standard sized bed pillows to stuff the cushion, or make a pad and stuff it with terylene (polyester) wadding.
Sewing thread to match backing fabric.
Tools and materials for preparing the canvas (see page 113), for blocking (see page 116) and for making up (see page 117).

WORKING THE DESIGN

Once you have prepared the canvas (see page 114), mount it on a frame (see page 114). Work the design in half cross stitch throughout using the yarns indicated in the chart on the previous page and the key to the left. Use the yarn straight from the skein, ie do not split it.

BLOCKING AND MAKING UP

When the design is complete, block if necessary (see page 116). Once the blocked work is completely dry, make it up into a cushion (see page 117). Alternatively, make a velvet frame, back the whole piece with hessian and use it as a wall hanging.

SHALL WE DANCE?

Inspired by *Ballet Rehearsal*, Edgar Degas (1834-1917)

Ballet Rehearsal by Edgar Degas (1834-1917)

Much of Degas' work was influenced by the new science of photography and he also shared with his contemporaries an interest in Japanese colour prints. Many of his paintings were created from a series of isolated studies which were then put together in a single composition. In his early years, Degas produced a number of portraits and works based on classical themes, much influenced by the old masters. His later works, following his meeting with Manet and the Impressionists, however, concentrated on contemporary subjects such as racing, ballet, café scenes and laundresses.

Degas was an academic, having trained for the law before entering the Ecole des Beaux-Arts. He was a superb draughtsman and despite opting for a reclusive lifestyle he was also a provocative conversationalist, well noted for his strong character and cutting tongue. A little like the master in this composition I should imagine.

OPPOSITE: Detail from *Shall We Dance?*

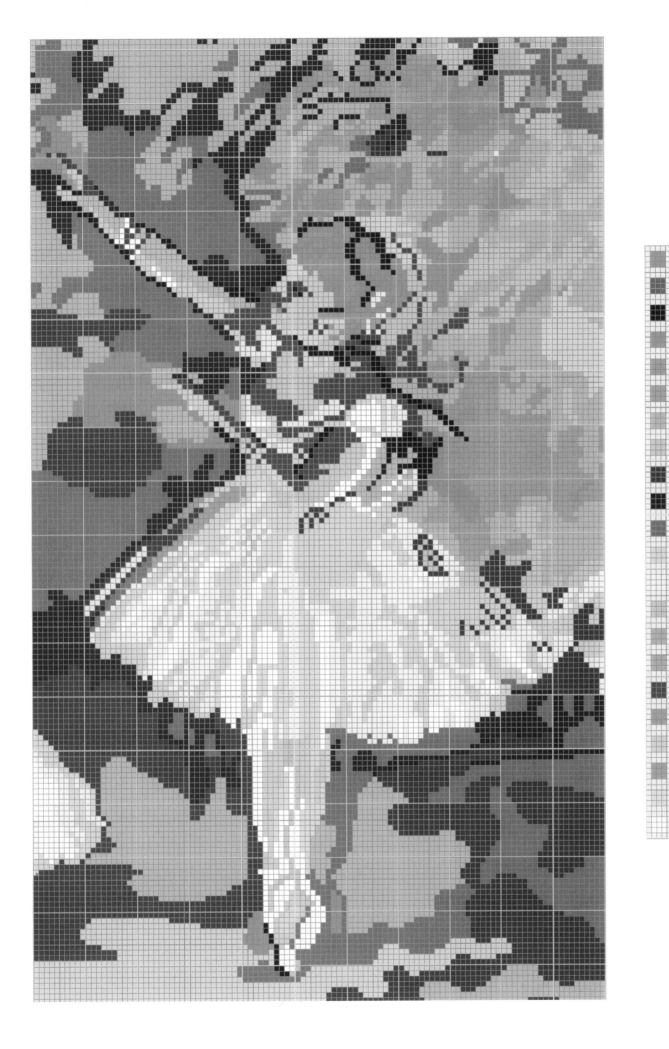

YARNS

10m skeins of Anchor Tapisserie Wool in the following colours and quantities:

Coffee	9368	× 1
Scarlet	8198	× 1
Charcoal	9768	× 2
Forest green	9078	× 2
Grey green	9076	× 1
Lime	9096	× 1
Aqua	8934	× 1
Kingfisher	8918	× 5
Petrol	8820	× 4
Grey blue	8738	× 3
Marine blue	8628	× 5
Sky blue	8776	× 4
Pale blue	8782	× 3
Mauve	8522	× 1
Coral	8416	× 1
Hyacinth	8604	× 1
Brown	9678	× 1
Beige	9490	× 1
Pink	8254	× 2
Light Beige	9324	× 1
Pale yellow	8038	× 1
Creamy pink	9612	× 2

MATERIALS

One piece of antique finish, 10 mesh, double canvas measuring 73.5 × 57cm (29 × 22½in). Actual design measures 63.5 × 47cm (25 × 19in).

10m skeins of Anchor Tapisserie Wool in the colours and quantities shown to the left.

Size 18 tapestry needle.

Tools and materials for preparing the canvas (see page 113), for blocking (see page 116) and for making up (see page 117).

WORKING THE DESIGN

Once you have prepared the canvas (see page 114), mount it on a frame (see page 114). Work the design in half cross stitch throughout using the yarns indicated in the chart on the previous page and the key to the left. Use the yarn straight from the skein, ie do not split it.

BLOCKING AND MAKING UP

When the design is complete, block if necessary (see page 116). Once the blocked work is completely dry, mount it on a board and the needlepoint will be ready to frame as required (see page 117).

PRETTY WOMAN

Inspired by *Luncheon of the Boating Party*, Pierre Auguste Renoir (1841-1919)

Luncheon of the Boating Party by Pierre Auguste Renoir (1841-1919)

I would love to have been present at the Café Guerbois in Paris, where Renoir, Monet, Sisley and Bazille sat drinking wine and discussing their latest discovery, Impressionism. But Renoir overcame hardship through profitable portrait painting and embarked on a different journey, the search for greater solidity in his work. He adapted his style to what he referred to as *manière aigre* (harsh and sour manner) and took for his favourite subjects, nudes and young girls doing various things. Of his nudes he commented "I never think I have finished a nude until I think I could pinch it" and in his paintings of young girls he sought a gentle manner: "Why shouldn't art be pretty, there are enough unpleasant things in the world?"

This design was originally produced as *Woman with Dog* by the needlework company Royal Paris, in France, who also sell kits for it. I have simply charted their interpretation for you.

OPPOSITE: *Pretty Woman* after a detail from *Luncheon of the Boating Party* by Pierre Auguste Renoir

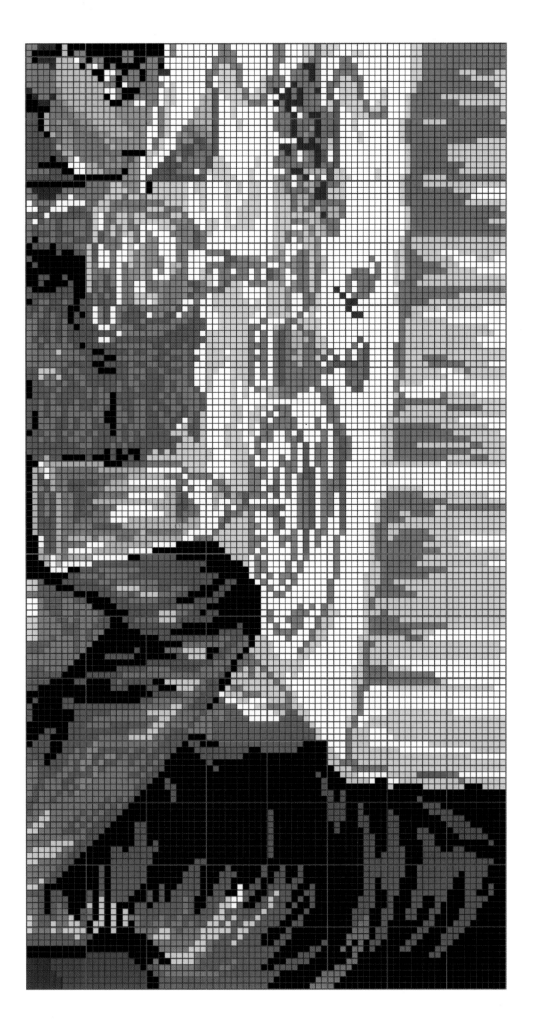

YARNS

10m skeins of Anchor Tapisserie Wool in the following colours and quantities:

Colour	Code	Qty
White	8000	× 4
Dark grey	9766	× 3
Mid grey	9776	× 3
Silver	8712	× 3
Black	9800	× 3
Tan	9526	× 1
Fawn	9636	× 1
Flame	8234	× 1
Old gold	8020	× 1
Yellow	8040	× 1
Blue	8630	× 1
Red	8238	× 1
Apricot	9502	× 1
Peach	9506	× 1
Coral	8306	× 1
Chestnut	9564	× 1
Mid green	9200	× 3
Dark green	9204	× 3

MATERIALS

One piece of antique finish, 10 mesh, double canvas measuring 57.5 × 47cm (22^{7}/$_{10}$ × 18^{1}/$_{2}$in). Actual design measures 47.5 × 37cm (18^{7}/$_{10}$ × 14^{1}/$_{2}$in).

10m skeins of Anchor Tapisserie Wool in the colours and quantities shown to the left.

Size 18 tapestry needle.

Tools and materials for preparing the canvas (see page 113), for blocking (see page 116) and for making up (see page 117).

WORKING THE DESIGN

Once you have prepared the canvas (see page 114), mount it on a frame (see page 114). Work the design in half cross stitch throughout using the yarns indicated in the chart on the previous page and the key to the left. Use the yarn straight from the skein, ie do not split it.

BLOCKING AND MAKING UP

When the design is complete, block if necessary (see page 116). Once the blocked work is completely dry, mount it on a board and the needlepoint will be ready to frame as required (see page 117).

BROWN SKINNED GIRL

Inspired by *Under the Pendanus*, Paul Gauguin (1848-1903)

Under the Pendanus by Paul Gauguin (1848-1903)

Gauguin was 35 years old before he took the step from business man and patron of the arts to artist. His true talent developed in the South Seas where the beautiful flowers inspired him. His style is described as poetic and symbolistic and he translated the simple lifestyle of the people he lived among into bold imagery using colour for its decorative and emotional effect rather than naturalistically.

While in Tahiti, Gauguin lived as a native and despite his poverty and ill health, produced some of his greatest works, including this one. Shortage of materials sometimes forced him to use his paint sparingly on coarse sacking as opposed to canvas but this necessity created a bold style which firmly established him.

I have produced Brown Skinned Girl as a footstool cover in the hope that one day I will be able to go to Tahiti and put my feet up.

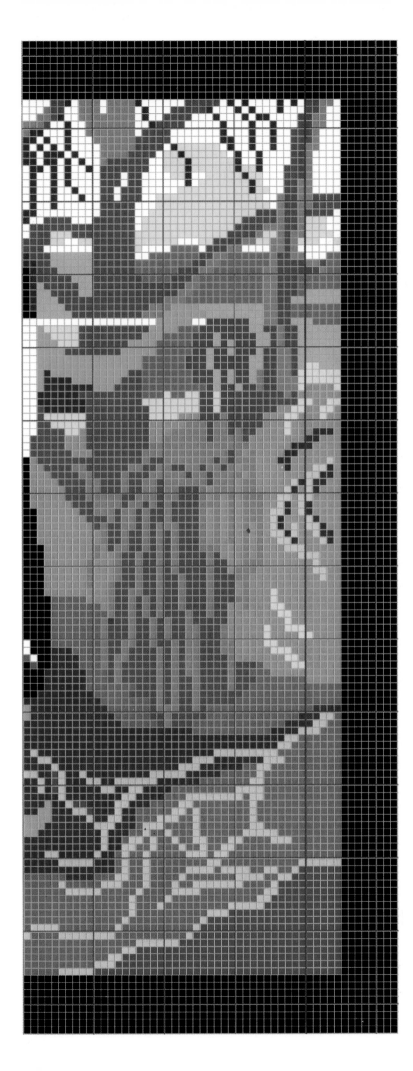
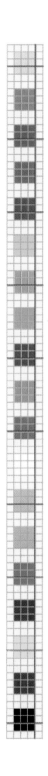

Brown Skinned Girl

YARNS

10m skeins of Anchor Tapisserie Wool in the following colours and quantities:

Colour	Code	
Silver	9672	× 1
Mushroom	9620	× 1
Dark green	8924	× 1
Burgundy	8512	× 3
Brown	9642	× 2
Gold	8022	× 1
Coral	8306	× 1
Tan	8104	× 1
Red	8196	× 1
Pinky mauve	8506	× 2
Royal	8610	× 1
White	8002	× 1
Aqua	8898	× 1
Hyacinth	8608	× 1
Green	9118	× 1
Dull mauve	8508	× 3
Mustard	8018	× 1
Chocolate	9648	× 1
Black	9800	× 4

MATERIALS

One piece of antique finish, 10 mesh, double canvas measuring 44.5 × 42cm (17½ × 16½in). Actual design measures 37 × 34cm (14½ × 13½in).

10m skeins of Anchor Tapisserie Wool in the colours and quantities shown to the left.

Size 18 tapestry needle.

Tools and materials for preparing the canvas (see page 113), for blocking (see page 116) and for stool base (see stockist information, page 119).

Staple gun.

32cm (12½in) square uncovered footstool (Note: I have designed this piece so that the border slightly overlaps the edges of a 32cm [12½in] square footstool ensuring that no bare canvas is left showing. If desired, the piece could also be used as a cushion front.)

WORKING THE DESIGN

Once you have prepared the canvas (see page 114), mount it on a frame (see page 114). Work the design in half cross stitch throughout using the yarns indicated in the chart on pages 96-7 and the key to the left. Use the yarn straight from the skein, ie do not split it.

BLOCKING AND MAKING UP

When the design is complete, block if necessary (see page 116). Once the blocked work is completely dry, stretch it over the top of the stool base. Staple the four corners to the underside then, stretching as you go, secure the centre of each side. Once you are satisfied that the positioning is correct, staple all the way round the stool at half inch intervals.

OPPOSITE: *Brown Skinned Girl* after *Under the Pendanus* by Paul Gauguin

SUNNY SUNNY DAY

Inspired by *Sunflowers*, Vincent van Gogh (1853-90)

Sunflowers by Vincent van Gogh (1853-90)

Van Gogh tried many jobs before he became a painter. He was a picture dealer, a theological student, an evangelist preacher, and a schoolmaster. His early paintings illustrated the sympathy he felt for the toil and poverty he encountered in his mission days. Later on, he teamed up with Gauguin and suffered various degrees of madness resulting in attacks on his fellow artist and the removal of a piece of his own ear.

Van Gogh's love of flowers inspired stunning and intense paintings and his famous Provençal sunflowers were a tribute to the peace and serenity he found while living among them. The painting this design is taken from hangs in the National Gallery in London.

I have chosen to mount this piece as the cover of a writing folder. It would, of course, make an excellent cushion or painting if required.

OPPOSITE: *Sunny Sunny Day* after *Sunflowers* by Vincent van Gogh

YARNS

10m skeins of Anchor Tapisserie Wool in the following colours and quantities:

	Colour	Code	Qty
	Dark brown	9666	× 1
	Rust	8164	× 2
	Mustard	8024	× 3
	Butter	8056	× 4
	Gold	8120	× 1
	Tangerine	8140	× 1
	Mid green	9198	× 1
	Dark green	9204	× 1
	Copper	8312	× 1
	Pale butter	8054	× 1
	Blue	8628	× 1
	Light green	9214	× 1
	Maize	8042	× 1
	Amber	8102	× 1
	Cream	8012	× 1

MATERIALS

One piece of antique finish, 10 mesh, double canvas measuring 35.5 × 41cm (14 × 16in). Actual design measures 25.5 × 29cm (10 × 11½in).
10m skeins of Anchor Tapisserie Wool in the colours and quantities shown to the left.
Size 18 tapestry needle.
Four pieces of medium weight cardboard measuring 25.5 × 29cm (10 × 11½in).
Two thicknesses of wadding (polyester) to match the cardboard.
Two sheets of decorative paper 30.5 × 36cm (12 × 14in).
One piece of heavyweight cotton fabric 38cm (15in) square.
Rubber based adhesive.
100cm (40in) braid.
Tools and materials for preparing the canvas (see page 113) and for blocking (see page 116).

WORKING THE DESIGN

Once you have prepared the canvas (see page 114), mount it on a frame (see page 114). Work the design in half cross stitch throughout using the yarns indicated in the chart opposite and the key to the left. Use the yarn straight from the skein, ie do not split it.

BLOCKING AND MAKING UP

When the design is complete, block if necessary (see page 116).

To make the folder, take one piece of the cardboard and glue a square of wadding on the top. Once the needlepoint is dry, mount it over the card and wadding in the normal way (see page 117).

Take a second piece of cardboard and cover one side with decorative paper, glueing the waste to the back. Repeat with the third piece of cardboard but when it is completed, lay the braid diagonally across the four corners and glue into position on the back only.

Take the fourth piece of cardboard and cover with fabric, leaving 8cm (3in) of material free at the left edge (covered side up). This will form the spine. Lay this face down and glue piece three (face up) on top of it. Glue pieces one and two together (wrong sides facing each other), sandwiching 5cm (2in) of the spine fabric between them.

ONLY JESTING

Inspired by *The Circus*, Georges Seurat (1859-91)

The Circus by Georges Seurat (1859-91)

Seurat's pointillism, or divisionism as he preferred to call it, resulted from a deep research into aesthetic and scientific treatises. He created vibrant and luminous images by placing colours side by side instead of mixing them (a technique very like the stitching process in needlepoint) although his ultimate aim was to find harmony. As such, he was considered a leader of the avant-garde and some 20 years following his untimely death at the age of 31, his work had a great influence on Picasso, Braque and Gris.

Unlike many of his contemporaries, Seurat came from a well-off family and never had to worry about earning a living. However, he was totally dedicated to his work and research and some said he literally worked himself to death.

Seurat painted *The Circus* in 1890-1, late in his short life, on a canvas measuring approximately 180 × 147cm (71 × 58in). It hangs in the Louvre in Paris. Working on a 10-mesh canvas, this needlepoint design measures 45.5 × 38cm (18 × 15in) and should hang very nicely in your living room.

OPPOSITE: *Only Jesting* after *The Circus* by Georges Seurat

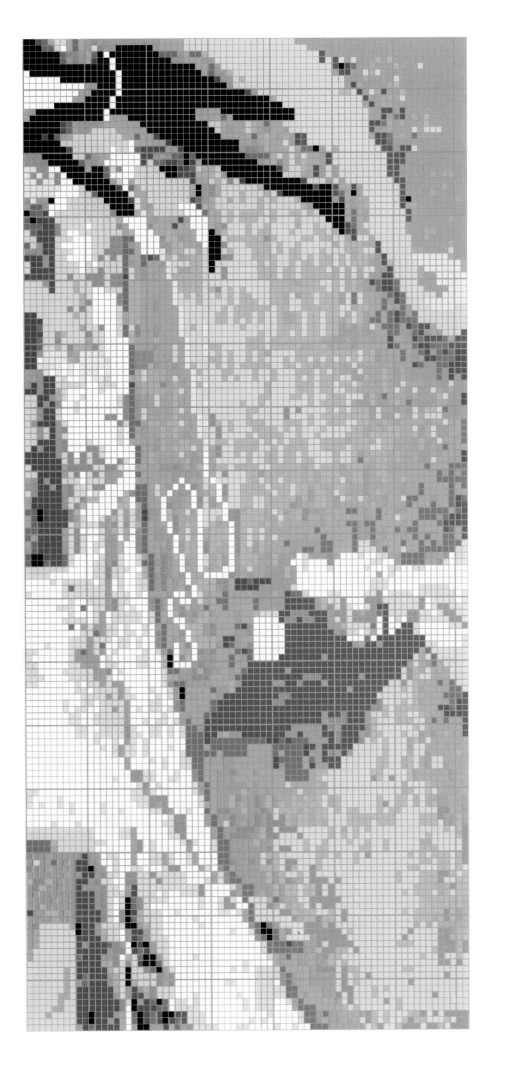

YARNS

10m skeins of Anchor Tapisserie Wool in the following colours and quantities:

Colour	Code	Qty
Mushroom	9676	× 4
Dark silver	9788	× 2
Brown	9662	× 2
Pale mushroom	9674	× 2
Beige	9656	× 2
Charcoal	9766	× 4
Coffee	9658	× 2
White	8000	× 4
Silver	9784	× 3
Black	9800	× 2
Yellow	8040	× 5
Rust	8312	× 2
Pinky cream	8294	× 1
Coral	8306	× 1
Orange	8140	× 1

MATERIALS

One piece of antique finish, 10 mesh, double canvas measuring 61 × 51cm (24 × 20in). Actual design measures 45.5 × 38cm (18 × 15in).

10m skeins of Anchor Tapisserie Wool in the colours and quantities shown to the left.

Size 18 tapestry needle.

Tools and materials for preparing the canvas (see page 113), for blocking (see page 116) and for making up (see page 117).

WORKING THE DESIGN

Once you have prepared the canvas (see page 114), mount it on a frame (see page 114). Work the design in half cross stitch throughout using the yarns indicated in the chart on the previous page and the key to the left. Use the yarn straight from the skein, ie do not split it.

BLOCKING AND MAKING UP

When the design is complete, block if necessary (see page 116). Once the blocked work is completely dry, mount it on a board and the needlepoint will be ready to frame as required (see page 117).

CAFÉ SOCIETY

Inspired by *Au Moulin Rouge*, Henri de Toulouse-Lautrec (1864-1901)

Au Moulin Rouge by Henri de Toulouse-Lautrec (1864-1901)

Henri de Toulouse-Lautrec was an aristocrat with a taste for the Paris café underworld. His growth was stunted in a sporting accident during his early teens but neither his grotesque appearance, his alcoholism nor his dissipated lifestyle interfered with his decision to work. Toulouse-Lautrec was strongly influenced by Degas and in his early teens he painted mainly sporting images. But from 1898, he concentrated on illustrations for theatre, circus, music-halls and brothels. His stark, emphatic images of gaslight society translate boldly into stitchery and make an interesting change from the subtly shaded artworks of the earlier schools.

The design shown here, *Café Society*, was inspired by Toulouse-Lautrec's *Au Moulin Rouge* and measures 40.5 × 30.5cm (16 × 12in). It works well here as a framed picture (see page 111) but it could just as easily be made up into a cushion which would complement a plain covered sofa.

OVERLEAF: *Café Society* after *Au Moulin Rouge* by Henri de Toulouse-Lautrec

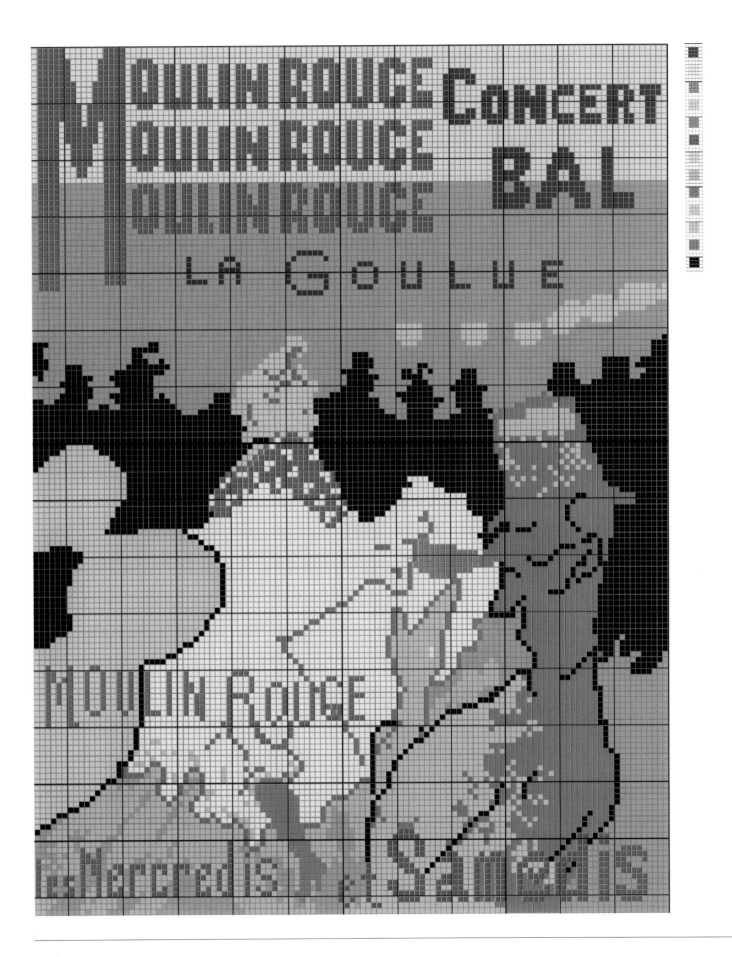

YARNS

10m skeins of Anchor Tapisserie
Wool in the following colours
and quantities:

	Colour	Code	Qty
■	Black	9800	× 3
■	Grey	9794	× 2
■	Light grey	9792	× 1
■	Yellow	8098	× 1
■	Green	9306	× 3
■	Maize	8040	× 1
■	Lime	9304	× 2
■	Red	8196	× 2
■	Mushroom	9620	× 1
■	Flesh	9522	× 1
■	Rose	8260	× 1
■	Cream	8052	× 2
■	Bottle	9208	× 1

MATERIALS

One piece of antique finish, 10
mesh, double canvas measuring
51 × 40.5cm (20 × 16in).
Actual design measures 40.5 ×
30.5cm (16 × 12in).
10m skeins of Anchor Tapisserie
Wool in the colours and
quantities shown to the left.
Size 18 tapestry needle.
Tools and materials for preparing
the canvas (see page 113), for
blocking (see page 116) and for
making up (see page 117).

WORKING THE DESIGN

Once you have prepared the
canvas (see page 114), mount it
on a frame (see page 114). Work
the main body of the design in
half cross stitch throughout
using the yarns indicated in the
chart on page 110 and the key to
the left. Use the yarn straight
from the skein, ie do not split it.
When this is complete, add the
lettering detail using straight
stitches in the colours indicated
on the photograph.

BLOCKING AND MAKING UP

When the design is complete,
block if necessary (see page 116).
Once the blocked work is
completely dry, mount it on a
board and the needlepoint will be
ready to frame as required (see
page 117).

TECHNIQUES

The basic technique involved in needlepoint is so simple that you can learn it in a minute. All the designs in this book are worked using one stitch, ie half cross stitch, although two of the designs, Café Society and Lullaby, have detail added over the top in small straight stitches. Because this is the case, do not be put off by what seems to be a complicated design. It isn't. Once you understand that each small square on the chart represents one stitch you will find all the designs plain sailing.

The same applies to size: some of the designs in this book are large and may seem a little daunting. The size of a piece relates to the number of holes to the inch on your canvas so, if you want to make a design smaller, simply buy a canvas that has more holes to the inch than those suggested.

For newcomers to needlepoint, I would recommend that you begin with the designs that contain large blocks of colour such as Stoney Silence or Café Society. Lady in Red and Only Jesting are produced for those with more experience because the colours change frequently to imitate the brushstrokes.

TOOLS

Before beginning any project, ensure that you have the following tools to hand:

1 A piece of canvas to the specified measurements.
2 The recommended yarns or a selection of your own choice.
3 At least half a dozen needles.
4 Scissors.
5 Masking tape.
6 The correct size of frame (if required).
7 A stitch unpicker.
8 A waterproof pen.

CANVAS

Needlepoint canvas is produced in various mesh sizes with specific numbers of holes or threads per 2.5cm (1in). For the purposes of this book, I have referred to mesh sizes as the number of holes to 2.5cm (1in) and not the number of threads. Mesh sizes can vary from as many as 32 holes per 2.5cm (1in) for extremely fine work such as petit point, to as few as 3 holes per 2.5cm (1in), which is used mainly for rugmaking. In some cases, petit point is used in the same design as half cross stitch. When this is the case I have used double thread canvas and worked into every hole instead of every other hole.

Most of the pieces in this book are worked on 10 mesh, a couple on 12 mesh and one, Lullaby, on 18 mesh. For this design I have used stranded cottons. You could change this to crewel (single strand) wools, if you choose.

There are two main types of quality canvas which are readily available. Single interlocked canvas, which is composed of a mesh of single interlocked threads, and double canvas, composed of double interlocked threads. There are also a number of cheaper types which are not interlocked and, unless your stitching is very even, avoid them as the loose weave could distort your work.

I have recommended double canvas for most of these designs because I think it gives better coverage to the yarns. However, it is only essential to use double canvas when you have to include some petit point detail. My choice of antique finish is also a matter of personal taste although, as a rule, you should work darker coloured designs on antique finish and lighter designs on white canvas.

PREPARATION

Cut canvas has raw edges which tend to catch on your hands, the wools and your clothes. For this reason it is a good idea to bind the edges of your canvas with masking tape before you begin stitching. This is obviously not necessary if you intend to work on a frame (see Frames, right).

As well as transferring your design on to the canvas with a waterproof pen (see Transferring the design to canvas, page 116), you might also want to divide your chart and canvas into quarters or eighths so that at all times you know where you are in your pattern.

The next question is "Where do I begin?" The traditional answer is that you either fold your canvas in half and in half again to find the centre point or you draw two lines across the centre, one vertical and one

horizontal to establish the same. Since I always allow 5cm (2in) of selvedge, I tend to start in the bottom left hand corner, 5cm (2in) up from the bottom and 5cm (2in) in from the left-hand edge. Whether you choose to start in the centre or in a corner, it is a good idea to have several needles handy, all threaded with different colours and to complete blocks of colour independently.

YARNS

Despite the glorious colours that are available, yarns, unfortunately, are not paints and, in order to chart these pieces so that they make sense, I have used solid strands of Anchor Tapisserie Wools which are widely available, of high quality and offer good colour density. If you want to achieve subtler effects, you could buy single strand crewel wools and use two or three shades together. The best crewel wools on the market are made by Appleton. Paterna also produce stranded yarns sold in small skeins and their colour range is extremely good.

Depending on the brand your local shop sells, you might find it more convenient to purchase DMC wools. Any reputable needlework shop will have shade cards for all these brands and by looking at these you can convert the colours from brand to brand and make your selection. One

word of warning, do not mix stranded wools with the Anchor or DMC single strand variety, the finish is different and this would make your work look messy.

The addresses for Anchor wools are listed under stockist information (see page 119) and also note that kits, some with printed canvases, containing all you need to make up the needlepoint, are available by mail order. Separate printed canvases for *The Last Supper* (The Final Feast), *Ballet Rehearsal* (Shall We Dance?), *Floral Composition* (Floral Tribute), *Flatford Mill* (Country Diary) and *Woman with Dog* (Pretty Woman), can also be purchased through needlework and departmental stores.

FRAMES

It makes a good deal of sense to produce your needlepoint on a frame. While it might be more convenient to work with your canvas on your lap this often leads to distortion and there is nothing worse than after weeks of work ending up with a canvas that bends and gathers in all directions. There are various types of frames available. For most projects, the straight-sided scroll frame is the most suitable. It consists of two pieces of doweling with attached webbing, on to which you sew the top and bottom of your canvas. These pieces of doweling then slot into two uprights, which hold them rigid. You then roll the canvas on to the doweling until the fabric is absolutely taut and cleverly secure the whole thing with the four wing nuts which are supplied with the frame. Frames come in a variety of widths so be sure you go to the shop armed with the correct measurements of your canvas. These frames are very reasonably priced and well worth the money.

Another type of frame is round and consists of two circles of wood with a screw across the top. You place one circle underneath your work and clamp the second section over your work, tightening the screw until your fabric is taut. These frames come in a large range of sizes and are useful when working small needlepoints. There are various stands available to support the frame. Some are made of beautiful polished wood, to enhance your living room, and some are stainless steel with the emphasis on adjustability to enhance your comfort.

NEEDLES

Tapestry needles are blunt ended and large-eyed and come in a range of sizes beginning at 13, for heavy work, and going up to 26 for very fine work. The important thing is that the needle should take the thickness of yarn easily, and fit through the hole on the canvas without pulling it out of shape. Specific needle sizes are given for each design, but the following will serve as a useful guide:

For 18 mesh canvas use size 22 needle.

For 13 and 14 mesh canvas use size 20 needle.

For 10 and 12 mesh canvas use size 18 needle.

For 6, 7 and 8 mesh canvas use size 16 needle.

STITCHES

HALF CROSS STITCH

All the designs in this book were produced in half cross stitch. The diagram below shows how the stitch is worked and the end result, which is a flat, slanted stitch over one row. Working the row from left to right, bring the needle up through the back of the canvas (1). Insert it in the hole one row up and one stitch along, ie diagonally (2). Bring the needle back through the canvas via the hole immediately below, ready for the next stitch (3).

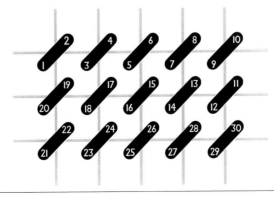

BACKSTITCH

The term backstitch means quite simply that you complete the straight stitch and then bring the needle up through the canvas at the point where the next stitch should end. Then insert from front to back at the point where the first stitch finished to form a straight line. It is used to add detail on top of your finished half cross stitch. For the strings of Lullaby, work backstitches over approximately six rows of half cross, in straight lines to form the strings. Backstitch is also used for the lettering on Café Society. Here you should vary the size of your individual stitches to create curves in the lettering where required.

PETIT POINT

Where petit point faces are required, I have provided you with a separate chart. It is recommended that you work the petit point detail first and then the half cross stitch that surrounds it. Petit point is worked in exactly the same way as half cross except you are treating the spaces between the strands of your double mesh

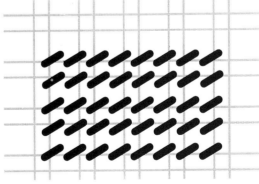

canvas as holes, ie you are making four petit point stitches for every one normal half cross.

READING THE CHARTS

The charts in this book are not drawn proportionally to the size of your canvas. However, each square represents a stitch in your canvas, so colour should be worked as closely as possible on the canvas to the areas allotted to them on the chart. It may help to take a photostat of the chart you are working on and cross off the rows as you complete them.

TRANSFERRING THE DESIGN TO CANVAS

While the designs can be read stitch for stitch from the printed charts, you might find it helpful to trace outlines of the images directly on the canvas. To do this, trace your outlines on tracing paper using a black crayon and then place your canvas over your tracing. With a coloured waterproof pen, overdraw the tracing directly onto the canvas. Using this method, you can substitute your own mix of colours.

CHANGING THE SIZE OF THE DESIGN

I have already mentioned that you can adjust the size of your design by choosing a different mesh canvas, ie less or more holes to the inch to make it

larger or smaller respectively. Alternatively, you could copy the design with tracing paper and then enlarge or reduce it at a photocopy shop before transferring the design as described above.

The traditional method of altering the size of a design is to trace it and then draw a grid of squares over it, thus defining which part of the design appears in each square. You then select your canvas, draw a grid of an equal number of squares onto it and then carefully draw in the design outline in waterproof pen, using the squares as a reference.

BLOCKING

You will need the following equipment: scissors, a wooden frame or board, a paper cutout of the correct finished measurement of your design, masking tape, upholstery or drawing pins, a waterspray or sponge and a hairdryer. If you have not worked your canvas on a frame, it is essential to block (or stretch) the needlepoint back into shape before making it up into a finished piece. Even if you have used a frame and it has not distorted I would still recommend blocking, if only to freshen the yarn appearance.

Begin by taping the paper cutout to the frame or board. Then place the finished canvas, wrong side up, on top of the

paper (moistening it very slightly first if it is badly distorted). Gently stretch the canvas to the outline on the cut out and pin it securely to the board, starting at the four corners, continuing along the four sides and using one pin every 2.5cm (1in).

Using a waterspray or damp sponge, dampen the work thoroughly (on the wrong side) and then leave until it is completely dry. (You can speed this up by gently playing a hairdryer across the surface.) Once dry, remove it from the frame.

UPHOLSTERING FURNITURE WITH NEEDLEPOINT

Many items of furniture would enjoy a new lease of life if used to display your beautiful needlepoint and there are flea markets and garage sales where you should easily find suitable pieces. However, for the purposes of this book, I commissioned Roger Newman, a local craftsman to make up pieces for me. If you live in Britain, he would be happy to make reproductions of these pieces for you. They include the firescreen (see pages 28-9), the cupid cupboard (see page 37), the writing box (see page 47) and the trunk (see pages 16-17). See page 119 for his address.

That Certain Smile chairback has been designed to fit a specific chair. Obviously, the dimensions of the tapestry may not suit the chair you wish to upholster. Before producing a needlepoint for a chairback or seat, your approach should be to make a template by cutting out the exact shape of your required seat or back in brown paper. You can then either increase the design by adding a border, or change the size of the mesh of your canvas so that you still have enough holes to complete the image but to a smaller overall size. Using this basic principle, you can size needlepoints to fit stool tops, work boxes or cupboard panels as you wish. Many of the designs in this book are shown as framed pieces but they can be adapted to suit different purposes, the choice being as wide as your imagination.

MOUNTING A DESIGN

If you intend framing a design, you will first have to mount it on board. To do this you will need the following: a piece of hardboard or acid free cardboard slightly larger than the finished work, some long pins, a reel of strong thread and a size 18 tapestry needle.

Place the work face down and lay the board on top of it. Fold in one long edge of canvas and pin this to the edge of the board at approximately 2.5cm (1in) intervals. Repeat along the other

long edge. Leaving the thread on the reel, thread your needle and lace the two long edges together from bottom to top. When this is complete, secure the ends of the cotton and repeat the process on the two short ends of your canvas.

MAKING A CUSHION

There are many ways of making up a cushion and lots of fabrics, braids and trims that can be used to highlight your needlepoint. Your choice of these depends entirely on personal taste.

The Child Angels and Lady In Red cushions have been centred on fabric with the corners mitred to create a framed effect. To reproduce this effect, cut four strips of fabric on the straight grain each measuring the length of one side of the needlepoint plus 1.5cm (⅝in) seam allowance.

For Child Angels your strip should be 10cm (4in) deep and for Lady In Red 14cm (5½in) deep. Join the first two strips diagonally at the corners with backstitch or a machined seam, leaving the seam allowance 1cm (½in), open at the inside edge. Trim the seam and press open. Repeat for the other three corners.

To insert the needlepoint in the centre, fold the inside edges of the fabric under and pin the fabric to the edge of the worked canvas, right sides facing. Join with an invisible seam.

Both the above cushions have also been piped. To make piping, cut a strip of the fabric to the

width of the circumference of the piping cord plus twice the seam allowance, and long enough to fit around the diameter of your cushion, joining the strips if necessary. Wrap the fabric strip around the cord face, right side out, and machine stitch close to the cord, using a zipper foot. Pin then tack (baste) the covered piping around the right side back edges of the cushion cover placing the cord inside the seamline. Cut the piping seam allowances at the corners so they will lie flat. Neatly join the ends of the piping cord together.

The Green Sleeves cushion has a rouched edge. This is made by cutting and joining strips of fabric twice the width of your intended frill plus 2.5cm (1in) seam allowance and twice the length of the diameter of your cushion. Fold the strip in half face outwards and run a thread along the seam allowance. Gather your frill by pulling in this thread until the strip fits neatly around the outside edges of your cushion. Join this to the back of your cushion as you would piping. Neatly join the two short edges.

The Angela cushion has been backed with a piece of fabric 2.5cm (1in) larger than the finished needlepoint. The edges have been folded in and stitched leaving an opening for a zip. The cushion has been trimmed with corded braid handsewn into place.

STOCKIST INFORMATION

Kits for the projects in this book are available by mail order. The kits contain the correct size canvas, appropriate yarns and a sewing needle. For mail order details and price list write to:

MELINDA COSS
Ty'r Waun Bach
Gwernogle
Dyfed
West Wales
SA32 7RY.

Anchor tapisserie wools and stranded cottons are available worldwide. For a list of local stockists write to:

COATS PATONS CRAFTS
PO Box McMullen Rd
Darlington

Co. Durham
DL1 1YQ.
or: *COATS AND CLARK INC.*
30 Patewood Drive
Suite 351
Greenville
South Carolina 29615.

The following printed, full-colour canvases are also available from Anchor stockists:
Degas' *Ballet Rehearsal*,
Constable's *Flatford Mill*,
Leonardo's *The Last Supper*.
The following designs are also available as printed canvases:
Van Spaendonck's, *Floral Composition*
Renoir's *Woman with Dog* (taken from *Luncheon of the Boating Party*).

These two canvases are produced by Royal Paris and are also available from Anchor stockists. However, if you have any trouble locating these write to:

ROYAL PARIS
Steiner Frères
100, Av du General De Gaulle
18500 Mehun-sur-Yevre
France.

For details on custom-made furniture please contact:

ROGER NEWMAN
Byrfon
Gwernogle
Dyfed
West Wales
SA32 7RY.

BOOKLIST

In the course of her research the author consulted the following books:

A Concise History of Painting From Giotto to Cezanne Michael Levey. Thames & Hudson (undated)

The Concise Oxford Dictionary of Art & Artists Edited by Ian Chilvers. Oxford University Press 1990

The Pre-Raphaelites Christopher Wood. Weidenfeld 1983

Fra Angelico at San Marco William Hood. BCA 1993

Degas by Himself Edited by Richard Kendall. Macdonald Orbis (London) 1988

Michelangelo and the creation of the Sistine Chapel Robin Richmond. Barrie & Jenkins 1992

Johannes Vermeer Celeste Brusati. Rizzoli Art Series (undated)

The Art of Lord Leighton Christopher Newall. Phaidon Press Ltd, 1990